Reporting on Poverty:
News Media Narratives and Third Sector Communications in Wales

Kerry Moore
Foreword by Sian Morgan Lloyd
and Kerry Moore

Cardiff University Press | Gwasg Prifysgol Caerdydd

Published by
Cardiff University Press
Cardiff University
PO Box 430
1st Floor, 30–36 Newport Road
Cardiff CF24 0DE
https://cardiffuniversitypress.org

First published 2020

Cover design by Hugh Griffiths
Front cover image: iStock.com/tirc83

Print and digital versions typeset by Siliconchips Services Ltd.

ISBN (Paperback): 978-1-911653-14-1
ISBN (XML): 978-1-911653-17-2
ISBN (PDF): 978-1-911653-18-9
ISBN (EPUB): 978-1-911653-15-8
ISBN (Kindle): 978-1-911653-16-5

DOI: https://doi.org/10.18573/book4

The full text of this book has been peer-reviewed to ensure high academic standards. For full review policies, see https://cardiffuniversitypress.org/site/research-integrity/

Suggested citation: Moore, K. 2020. *Reporting on Poverty: News Media Narratives and Third Sector Communications in Wales.* Cardiff: Cardiff University Press. DOI: https://doi.org/10.18573/book4. License: CC BY-NC-ND 4.0

To read the free, open access version of this book online, visit https://doi.org/10.18573/book4 or scan this QR code with your mobile device:

Contents

List of Tables

List of Figures

Foreword

Kerry Moore & Sian Morgan Lloyd

The pressures and problems encapsulated in the term 'crisis of journalism' have been widely discussed by media and communications scholars. There are evident and evolving challenges impacting journalists and the working contexts in which they do their jobs. Despite this, a profound need remains for journalistic scrutiny to shine a light on social inequality and maintain an incisive focus on social affairs.

It is important to make sense of intense shifts impacting the wealth and standards of living within our communities, including growing inequalities in income, insecure employment, inadequate housing, and an increasingly threadbare safety net of welfare provision. Most people would agree that the fact that child poverty, hunger, homelessness, disparities in health and education are major and escalating issues in 21st-century Britain is a travesty.

Journalism plays a fundamental and necessary role in how 'we', as a society, recognise and understand these issues – what 'we' are saying and doing about them and, crucially, how those in positions of power and influence to affect them (at Westminster, in Cardiff, in local authorities, in business) are responding to them.

Wales is a diverse society of urban and rural lifestyles, Welsh- and English-language-speakers and cultural backgrounds. It is also relatively poor compared to most areas of the United Kingdom and other EU member states. The interests and experiences of people in Wales deserve to be recognised and well represented in the public discourse. Political devolution is recent and remains in a state of evolution and development and in this scenario, because a considerable proportion of the population look elsewhere for news and information, the media in Wales faces significant issues of identity and sustainability.

It is impossible to accurately research the media in Wales without including Welsh-language output. Welsh-language media is an integral part of the journalistic landscape in Wales and includes robust news and current affairs coverage of social affairs, often featuring individuals and areas of Wales that would not otherwise be covered in much depth or even at all. As a unique opportunity for conceptual collaboration between scholarly practice and academic research in journalism, our project is distinctive and innovative in exploring the dynamics of a bilingual media industry and its interactions, in Welsh and English, with the wider communications industry. It is perhaps surprising that, in exploring how an issue of great contemporary social significance is considered, interpreted and reported on in the two official languages of Wales, the project has been pioneering. Yet it is – there is currently no other scholarship in our field like this, and as such we hope it is valuable not only to journalism and media scholars but also for teaching and learning more broadly in the social sciences.

Our research addresses vital questions surrounding how poverty, social inequality and injustice are handled in the public discourse at a vital and critical conjuncture. To analyse news during the 2016 referendum campaign (and its aftermath) on Britain's membership of the EU was to witness how a moment of such intense uncertainty, political polarisation and, at times, surreal messaging presented problems for a journalism seeking to fairly represent both sides and make sense of what leaving or remaining would mean for their audiences. Rigorously interrogating news coverage at the time of the Tata Steel crisis also engaged us with an unfolding industrial history in Wales, contextualising ordinary people's livelihoods, hopes and fears with past experiences of sociopolitical conflict and economic challenge. These news narratives reported major moments of turmoil in Wales but equally indexed wider (national and global) political, social and economic crises. Exploring how, in practice, journalism and communications work can connect the local to the global, reporting relevant stories that make sense of such complex wider framings for poverty, is one of the most significant interventions of this book.

That participants from the journalism and third sector communications industries should be willing to take a step back from their everyday practice and reflect upon the opportunities and challenges inherent to their work on poverty (and upon their interactions with one another) for the purposes of research is testament to the importance they attribute as professionals to this subject. It has enabled a crucial dialogue to begin in Wales about how those professionals see their role in the public discourse, the role 'we' as a society may need them to do and the possibilities and impediments to bringing these things to pass – both now and in the future. This is a live and ongoing conversation facilitated by our research, but one that depends and will continue to depend upon the goodwill, expertise and engagement of journalists, third sector communications professionals and others as we face a rather bleak immediate future in Wales for those experiencing poverty.

A journalism that engages in a meaningful and objective fashion with poverty, which represents the complexity of poverty's economic, social and political causes with clarity, and which tells the story of its intense social harm, is essential. Journalism that holds the powers that be to account is the kind of journalism that, in all likelihood, most people who are concerned about social inequality would like to see. Reporting on poverty in such a way may be no mean feat, but, in a context of intensifying levels and experiences of poverty during a period of unprecedented political uncertainty, the need for it to do so could not be greater.

Acknowledgements

This project was commissioned by Oxfam Cymru and a coalition of key third sector organisations (Street Games Wales, Welsh Council for Voluntary Action, the Church in Wales, the Muslim Council of Wales, Cymorth Cymru, Tai Pawb, Community Housing Cymru, Christian Aid and Save the Children), each of which seeks to promote fair, accurate and progressive reporting of poverty issues in Wales.

It was also funded by three grants from the Cardiff University Research Opportunities Programme (CUROP), which allows undergraduate students to work with staff as research interns, and a further two grants for research impact: one from the Cardiff School of Journalism, Media and Culture (JOMEC) and one ESRC Impact Acceleration award.

Although I am individually responsible for the writing of this book and leading the project upon which it has been based, readers will note the abundant references throughout the book to 'our research'. The 'Exploring the Narrative' research project upon from which this book has been developed has enabled a unique and rich collaboration between colleagues in the Cardiff School of Journalism, combining academic and scholarly journalistic expertise. Working alongside co-investigator Sian Morgan Lloyd (JOMEC Lecturer, leading the School's Welsh-language provision) has been an incredibly supportive, collegiate and (I hope) mutually enriching experience. Working together has allowed us, crucially, to engage genuinely with current issues and experiences of journalistic practice and communications, to ask meaningful questions that make sense to professionals working in those industries in Wales, and to do so bilingually, in Welsh and in English. It has also allowed us to support and train a team of researchers working in both languages – Dr Alida Payson, Dr Gerraint Whittaker, Sandra Hicks, Sophie Jackson, Tanya Harrington and Elen Davies – whose significant contributions were recognised in the co-authorship of the research report preceding this book. I am also immensely grateful to JOMEC colleagues Glynn Mottershead and Martin Chorley, who provided invaluable expertise and support developing our tools for the analysis of online news; to Sian Powell, who supported the development of the project in its early stages; to Manon Edwards Ahir for her insightful comments, encouragement and support of our first project event; and to Jane Bentley and Simon Williams for enthusiastically engaging their students with the research and challenging me throughout to reflect upon its meaning for future practice in journalism and communications.

I would like to extend my gratitude to journalist and broadcaster Jackie Long for her encouragement and for generously giving her time as a guest speaker at our networking event in Cardiff in April 2017, and to Randeep Ramesh, chief leader writer of *The Guardian*, for doing the same at our 'Reporting on Poverty' event in JOMEC in November 2018. I am indebted to all who gave their time to making these events a success, including Richard Speight, Linda Mitchell, India Pollack, Andrea Byrne, Paul Rowland, Eurgain Haf, Deanndre Wheatland, and to the news media and third sector professionals who have taken part in the project in various ways. Finally, heartfelt thanks to Casia William, former media and communications officer at Oxfam (now at the Disasters Emergency Committee) for initiating and actively supporting this research in its bilingual form from its inception and without whom this project would not have come to fruition.

CHAPTER 1

Why Study News Media Narratives on Poverty?

What poverty *is* and how it should be understood have long been the object of political debate. In any historical moment, a range of ideas about poverty will be constructed and be seen differently by different groups in society. Captured and represented as 'facts' in the news, however, some ideas about poverty will become more powerful than others, helping to shape what is recognised to be 'common sense'. Particular interpretations of poverty as an issue may be favoured in news narratives, which reinforce (or challenge) common understandings. News narratives may also communicate potentially strong feelings or moral judgements about the way society is, or should be, dealing with poverty. As such, they can play a central role in reflecting and reproducing, challenging and transforming ideas on poverty. In these ways, news narratives potentially influence policymakers and public opinion, as well as shaping how poverty may be encountered and experienced by ordinary people.

This book is about 'unpacking' current news media narratives on poverty: it is about understanding how and why poverty is represented in the news media in the way that it currently is, and exploring how news coverage on poverty can be as accurate and as meaningful as it can be in representing the stories, issues and experiences of poverty in Wales today. Firstly, the study analyses news content featuring poverty, comparing print, online and broadcast media in Wales in English and Welsh to produce an evidence base about the features and patterns of poverty coverage. Secondly, it explores journalistic practices in reporting poverty issues. It examines the information needs, opportunities and institutional and cultural challenges encountered by journalists and editors currently working in news and current affairs. Lastly, the report considers the communications practices of the third sector in Wales, including their relationships with journalists. It outlines some of the opportunities, constraints and

---

How to cite this book chapter:
Moore, K. 2020. *Reporting on Poverty: News Media Narratives and Third Sector Communications in Wales.* Pp. 1–10. Cardiff: Cardiff University Press. DOI: https://doi.org/10.18573/book4.a. License: CC-BY-NC-ND 4.0

pressures the third sector faces in responding to or seeking to influence news media narratives on poverty as part of their work. In developing an in-depth picture of the professional aims, pressures and priorities currently shaping poverty reporting and communications practices, the research provides a resource for mutual understanding between journalists and third sector professionals in the interest of producing news narratives on poverty in Wales that are as representative, meaningful and accurate as possible.

Poverty in the UK

Researchers and policymakers have long recognised the need to demonstrate the significance of poverty as a social issue, moving beyond understanding poverty simply in terms of the minimum necessary income of individuals (see, for example Townsend, 1979). As such, although absolute poverty – the inability to afford the basics to survive, feed, clothe and house oneself – remains an important measure, public discussions on the social significance of poverty usually refer to *relative poverty* – low incomes measured in relation to average incomes. The Bevan Foundation, a leading charity working on poverty research in Wales, defines the experience of poverty to be when a person's resources 'are well below their minimum needs, including the need to take part in society' (Bevan Foundation, 2016: 6). Understanding poverty as a social issue, affecting multiple aspects of people's lives, relationships and opportunities, constitutes an essential starting point for this book.

Poverty in the UK is widespread (Marsh et al., 2017). If we consider that the UK remains one of the largest economies in the world as measured by GDP, official relative poverty figures in the UK are striking: 21% of the population in the UK (around 14 million people) live in relative poverty, and a higher proportion of people live in poverty in Wales (23%, 690,000 people) (Barnard, 2018; Statistics for Wales, 2017a: 4).[1] These rates have recently been quite stable; however, experts forecast relative poverty in Wales to rise to around 27% (around 40% for child poverty) over the next few years.

Whilst rates of poverty generally may be stable, they mask demographic variations and tangible changes in the conditions and experiences of poverty. For example, according to the Joseph Rowntree Foundation, across the UK 52% of people in poverty are in working families. In Wales, the group experiencing the highest rates of poverty is working-age families with children, whereas pensioners experience the lowest rates (Barnard, 2018: 4; Tinson et al., 2016). Unemployment – widely discussed as a factor directly contributing to poverty – has ostensibly fallen in recent years. However, in certain areas of Wales, such as Merthyr Tydfil and Blaenau Gwent, rates run well above those of the UK average (7.3% and 6.7%, respectively), and across Wales are higher amongst 16- to 24-year-olds (13.1%) (Bevan Foundation, 2018: 3). Moreover, unemployment figures do not account for the 21% of all working-age adults in the UK classified as having relative low income[2] (McGuinness, 2018: 12). Indeed, in-work poverty has become an increasingly serious issue. Low wages are often compounded by insecure conditions, including casualisation, unpredictable working hours (e.g. zero hours contracts), precarious and short-term contracts and agency-mediated self-employment lacking employment rights. In addition, changes to the welfare benefits and working tax credits systems have impacted the income levels of many households, exacerbated by errors, unpredictability and delays in the payments of Universal Credit, Employment Support Allowance (ESA) and Personal Independence Payments (PIP) as these have been rolled out.[3] Increasing risks of poverty – for those in as well as out of work – are driven by 'reductions to working age benefits, rising living costs (particularly for housing) and poor quality work' (Barnard, 2018: 1). This mix of low-paid, insecure work, cuts to social welfare, and rising costs of living, means poverty is both increasing and changing shape. In this climate, third sector organisations have played an increasing role in dealing with the fallout of these changes, plugging new gaps in the welfare provision and responding to expanding demand for their services from those in need.

Sharply rising inequality, living costs and debt have meant steadily increasingly numbers of people have been 'squeezed', exposed to hardship and vulnerable to social exclusion as their living conditions fall short of publicly accepted norms. Relative poverty figures also fail to capture what has been termed 'deprivation poverty' – a measure of basic material and social necessities for minimum living conditions as understood by the public. According to a major 2012 survey on living standards, 'more and more families in Britain face little more than a hand-to-mouth existence', with around a third of people in the UK found to live in multiply deprived households (Gordon et al., 2013: 16; Lansley & Mack, 2015: xiii). The symptoms of deprivation can be traced in the palpable rise in the use of food banks (emergency food aid) in recent years. According to UN figures reported by the Food Foundation and End Hunger UK groups, an estimated 10.1% of people in the UK experienced food insecurity in 2014 and over three million people in the UK counted as 'food insecure' between 2014 and 2016 (Goodwin, 2018). Similarly, fuel (or energy) poverty has become more commonplace, with recent estimated figures suggesting 11% of UK households, and 30% in Wales, struggle to adequately heat their homes[4] (Barton & Hough, 2016; Department for Business Energy and Industrial Strategy, 2017). The extent to which news media coverage of poverty has kept pace with these changes, capturing their lived realities and narrating the meaning of poverty for people in Wales today, is a key question addressed by this book.

At the very sharpest end, persistent poverty has been increasing, affecting approximately 4.6 million people across the UK (7.3% of the UK population) (ONS, 2017).[5] Homelessness has also become much more visible, with rough sleeping on the rise (by up to 30% in Wales in 2015–16) (Ministry of Housing Communities and Local Government, 2018; Statistics for Wales, 2017b; UK Government, 2017). The widely reported deaths of two young people sleeping rough in Cardiff during the bitter winter months of 2017–18 tragically highlighted this issue in Wales (ITV News, 2018; Mosalski, 2017). However, despite reportedly improved practices on homelessness prevention brought by the Housing (Wales) Act 2014, local authorities have reported 'significant' rises in statutory homelessness (those seeking homelessness assistance), and the scale of 'hidden homelessness' in Wales, including 'sofa surfing', other informal assistance and overcrowded households, remain difficult to assess (Fitzpatrick et al., 2017: 7).

Experiences of poverty are, of course, never fully captured by the statistics, however detailed or specific. Access to assets and resources, such as decent housing, food, fuel and other material necessities, tells an important story, but so does access to community or social networks as well as less tangible resources such as social hope, aspirations, ambitions and expectations for the future. In addition to coping with surviving without enough to live on, people experiencing poverty may also face cultures of humiliation, feelings of wounded pride, fear and despair and the deprivation of voice and social capital (Lister, 2004). These personal, emotional and symbolic experiences are woven through the social consequences of poverty – its impacts upon physical and mental health, educational attainment and culture, in social isolation or exclusion (including digital exclusion) and other chronic problems such as addiction or debt (Hirsch, 2007). The feelings of persistent anxiety and insecurity inherent to experiences of existing on low incomes, derived from precarious employment and social security benefits in an era of austerity, can be profound and deep-rooted (Pemberton et al., 2017).

Lived experiences of poverty may also be shaped by particular cultural and gendered experiences in turn, and conditioned by age or stage of life (Threadgold et al., 2007). Certain groups are at particular risk, such as people with a disability or mental health problem. Indeed, 26% of those in poverty in Wales have a disability (Tinson et al., 2016: 34). Other particularly vulnerable groups include looked after children and those leaving care, asylum seekers and refugees (Bevan Foundation, 2016). Whilst urban poverty may be more visible to most, rural poverty is an especially important issue in Wales, where particular problems associated with access to services, decent affordable housing, low wages and access to opportunities can be especially acute (Bevan Foundation, 2010).

Policy responses to poverty

Policy responses to poverty depend upon how its causes and consequences are understood. These tend to oscillate between societal and structural explanations and factors conditioned by individual or personal behaviours (Lansley & Mack, 2015). Policy areas related to tackling poverty focus in different ways on employment, working incomes, support services and benefits, education and training, health, housing or other community or cultural interventions. Many services in these areas are delivered by third sector organisations working independently and/or contracted by the state. However, with devolved government in Wales, political responsibilities for tackling poverty and its related issues are divided between Westminster, Cardiff Bay and local government. Whilst some of these areas, such as education, health and housing, fall within the remit of the Welsh Government and local councils, other significant policy responsibilities, including work and benefits, as well as the majority of tax raising powers remain with Westminster.[6] As such, there can be political tensions between the respective bodies. There can also sometimes be a disconnect between policy aims and power over actions designed to meet them, as evidenced by the Welsh Government's announcement in 2016 that UK government targets to eradicate child poverty by 2020 could not be achieved (BBC News, 2016). European Union interventions, such as investments in infrastructure in Wales's most deprived areas, have also added a layer of complexity to the question of responsibility for poverty and deprivation. In interpreting the 2016 referendum results, some commentators have noted that low-income households and those living in areas of high unemployment were much more likely to vote leave than those living in areas with high incomes or low unemployment (Armstrong, 2017: 5; Goodwin & Heath, 2016)

Poverty narratives – what we already know...

Contemporary political discourses on poverty will, almost inevitably, be woven through news media narratives as they report on political agendas, speeches, decisions and policies. The language choices politicians or journalists use in their narratives can be (and often are) 'loaded' in ways that encourage certain conditions of poverty to be taken as natural, questioned or judged. For example, since 2010, a strategy focusing on 'troubled families' and poor parenting has arguably cast poverty more as an outcome of behavioural shortcomings (Lansley & Mack, 2015). More recently, political talk about 'just about managing' families or those 'left behind' have similarly dealt with economic position primarily through the recognition of individuals' conduct, even if the experience and/or fear of poverty is apparently highlighted in an apparently more sympathetic, familiar and relatable light. Such strategies for talking about poverty and economic deprivation focus attention less upon the systemic factors and policy decisions structuring those experiences and more upon individual behaviour and morality. How journalists engage with such political labels and other language referencing poverty is important because this influences which powerful presuppositions about poverty are held to account critically or become naturalised and embedded within the wider public discourse.

Indeed, we know from previous research that public understanding and beliefs about significant social issues are, to some degree at least, conditioned by news agendas. Whilst the power of news is not necessarily that it tells audiences *what* to think, it does inform audiences what it may be important to think *about* (McCombs, 2004). Low levels of coverage may mean that poverty becomes a 'hidden' issue. When stories do hit the headlines, how poverty is identified, our expectations about what it looks like, how it is experienced and who is experiencing it are potentially brought into focus. The evidence we have on public beliefs about poverty in Britain show that people tend to be ill-informed. For example, many people believe that only a very small minority of people are poor (Clery, 2013) and that the elderly (rather than those of working age) are most at risk of poverty (Eurobarometer, 2010).

We also know that the public can hold morally judgemental views towards those experiencing poverty (Baumberg et al., 2013). Although public understandings vary, they tend to be characterised by limited number of 'cultural models' which predispose the public towards profoundly different feelings or beliefs about the issues at stake and the appropriate actions to address them. Thus, assuming poverty to be a consequence of 'cultural-behavioural predispositions' casts 'self-help' as a logical response, whereas understanding poverty as 'structurally determined' is more likely to suggest 'state interventions' to help those in need (Volmert, Pineau & Kendall-Taylor, 2017). With this in mind, and in light of the campaigning issues and outcome of the 2016 EU referendum, it is interesting to note that UK respondents in the Eurobarometer survey were more likely than those of any other country to identify immigration as a cause of poverty (37%). Poll respondents ranked immigration as the cause of poverty above 'the implementation of poor or badly suited policies' (30%), 'insufficient economic growth' (28%), 'pursuit of profit' (21%), 'the global financial system' (24%) and 'the inadequacy of the social protection system' (18%) (Eurobarometer, 2010: 67–68).

Because the news media plays a central role in shaping everyday narratives surrounding the issues that matter, those surrounding poverty will be limited by the ways in which poverty is regularly 'framed' in coverage – the dominant ways in which ideas about poverty are classified, presented and talked about. Media research has repeatedly highlighted how historical tropes distinguishing the 'deserving and undeserving poor' persist in contemporary media culture (Baumberg et al., 2013; Golding & Middleton, 1982; Robert, Shildrick & Furlong, 2014). In recent times, research has shown that the British national press tends to privilege individualising and rationalising frames over the social justice framing of poverty (Redden, 2011). Contextualising poverty in this way makes it more easy to blame people experiencing poverty for their own misfortune and for derogatory stereotypes casting the poor as 'degenerate', lacking 'taste', 'choice incompetent' or unnecessarily reliant on the state as 'welfare scroungers' (Bauman, 2004; Bourdieu, 2012 (1984)). Stigmatising caricatures, such as 'the chav', have been predicated on such media representations, and arguably enable economic and social injustices to be more easily overlooked or dismissed (Jones, 2011; Tyler, 2013). Such stereotypes have too often functioned as dominant cultural norms, helping to shape politically expedient images of poverty and why it exists. Designating poverty as a consequence of individual behaviour, values or inadequacy also serves vested interests in hierarchies of privilege and the reinforcement of economic and social inequalities. Discourses articulating myths of meritocracy, for example, have pervaded the rhetoric of mainstream politicians of the centre-right and centre-left in recent years, as well as becoming embedded in popular cultural narratives of social aspiration, celebrity and wider media culture (Bloodworth, 2016; Littler, 2018).

Poverty need not necessarily be mentioned explicitly or discussed directly for ideas about it to be implied or inferred. For example, cues and connotations may also be taken from references to place, such as 'the inner city', 'the suburbs' or specific areas associated with industrial decline, and these too can invoke powerful ideas and images associated with poverty and other social inequalities because they are deeply embedded in cultural norms and expectations (Crossley, 2017; Wacquant, 2008). It is therefore all the more important that the news media's role in (re)producing, sustaining or challenging those norms is better understood. To do this, we need to both pay close attention to the coverage itself and examine how the routines and practices of journalism can shape the coverage of poverty (Schneider, 2013). It is not necessarily or primarily the intentions of individual journalists that shape poverty news. In reporting poverty, journalists may be influenced by professional values and ideals, such as objectivity and balance, but they will also be exposed to the dominant existing cultures of understanding of the issue as well as targeted public relations communications of government and other organisations, including pressure groups and charities. Journalists reporting poverty news will also be subject to the particular styles and editorial lines of their news outlets, to professional codes as well as the routine, everyday opportunities and constraints faced in their reporting practice.

It remains important, therefore, to take into account how journalistic routines, formats, cultural norms and contextualising pressures on the news medium, including regulatory frameworks may play a role in the production of different types of news content. Across the national press, at least to some degree, there is diversity in ideological stance and editorial orientation, even if the scale of circulation and readership of right-wing titles do considerably exceed those of liberal titles. As such, most commentators would expect to see a qualitative difference on issues of inequality and social (in)justice, for example, between the coverage of the *Daily Mail* and that of *The Guardian*. Unlike the print news media, broadcast news in the UK is subject to regulation requiring impartiality in its coverage as part of its public service remit (even if these ideals may not always be met) (Lewis & Cushion, 2019) That said, it remains important to acknowledge that, even in the context of what is often called a 'crisis' in contemporary journalism (driven by falling print newspaper circulations and uncertainty surrounding sustainable alternative economic models for news in a digital age), the daily news agendas of national newspapers continue to be considered to heavily influence those of broadcasters and other news media (Cushion et al., 2018). However, broadcast, and especially television news media, may harness symbolic power more readily than other formats, representing aesthetic qualities of stories through powerful visual codes and conventions in ways that mobilise ideas, attitudes and feelings, in ways that potentially encourage spectating audiences to engage with or distance themselves from news subjects (Chouliaraki, 2006, 2013).

We may also expect to see differences in the coverage of poverty between national and local and regional news due to variances in the news values and styles prioritised by journalists and editors (Harcup & O'Neill, 2017; Jenkins & Nielsen, 2019). For example, it may generally be considered more typical that local news will focus on appealing to 'the popular' (for example, through personal, sensational or human interest stories) over ideals of 'quality' (such as in-depth social analysis of issues) (Nielsen, 2015), producing content that tends to be reductionist and depoliticised as a result (Bourdieu, 1996). However, it's important to acknowledge that the distinction between these ideals in practice are often not so clear cut (Franklin & Murphy, 1991; Franklin & Richardson, 2002). For example, in their research with local journalists across four European countries, Jenkins and Nielsen note how interviewees considered that 'quality journalism should entertain readers, appeal to emotion, and reflect the experiences of ordinary people, elements often associated with popular journalism' (Jenkins & Nielsen, 2019: 7). Indeed, the notion that focusing on everyday life, emotions and what Costera Meijer calls 'intimate journalism' should not generally be seen as characteristic of 'serious' or 'quality' journalism has long been challenged as myopic, especially by feminist and other critical scholars (Macdonald, 1998; Meijer, 2001; Wahl-Jorgensen, 2018). Engaging with how news affects ordinary people and their communities in their everyday realities and experiences also seems to address audience expectations that local news will 'embody communitarian values' (Nielsen, 2015) and be more constructive and less negative than news more generally. Indeed, arguably, the notion that local journalists should, as Rasmus Kleis Nielsen notes, 'care about the community to understand and appreciate its values, and, crucially, to prioritise solutions as much as problems in their coverage' (Nielsen, 2015: 12) could be seen as one indicator of 'quality' in journalism more generally.

With its capacity to offer textual and audio-visual content, online news allows for some of the formal distinctions between 'legacy' news formats to collapse or converge. However, with much more competition vying for the attention of audiences in a digital news environment, real-time data and audience metrics, different and specific pressures may face journalists producing online news about social issues. For example, concerns about 'clickbait' (news driven by curiosity generating techniques primarily intended to compel audiences to 'click' on content links) reintensify concerns about the supposed quality-diminishing effects of popular news styles and formats, rearticulating them with the technologically enabled pressures of possibilities online for attracting, monitoring and responding to audience attention, often more or less in real time. In social issue reporting, it is not difficult to imagine how the kinds of negative stereotypes that have historically been attached to people experiencing poverty could be exacerbated in such a pressured environment, through headlines deploying either 'undue certainty' (e.g. '10 things that will change your life!') or 'deliberate ambiguity' (e.g. 'You won't believe what happened next...!'), and tendencies media scholars have generally identified with clickbait, such as 'simplification', 'spectacularisation' and 'provoking content' that fuel concerns about its impact on journalistic quality (Blom, 2015; Kuiken, Schuth, Spitters & Marx, 2017; Molyneux & Coddington, 2019; Rowe, 2011; Tenenboim, 2015). On the other hand, the comparatively flexible space and multimedia possibilities for online news arguably also offer the potential for more in-depth feature or investigative journalism to be published, allowing both 'big' social issues, such as poverty, and everyday life stories consequent to those issues to more readily be explored and covered well by journalists. Online pressures towards more 'audience-oriented' approaches that potentially take the 'domain of everyday life' more seriously may also influence how journalists view their roles and relationships with news consumers as, for example, 'the service provider, connector, and guide' (Hanitzsch & Vos, 2018: 12; Jenkins & Nielsen, 2019: 4).

The present study provides an opportunity to compare between different types of news in its coverage of poverty and how journalists working across a range of roles and organisations in the industry in Wales reflect upon their practice reporting on this subject. In recent years, the value of reflecting upon journalistic practice in reporting poverty has been recognised by others, with some good practice guidelines emerging on reporting poverty in the UK (for example, Church Action on Poverty & National Union of Journalists, 2016; Seymour, 2009). However, this book represents the first systematic investigation of bilingual poverty coverage and reporting practices in Wales, and the first project assessing the role of media communications and experiences of journalists with the third sector. In the next chapter, we outline in detail our methodology for the study as a whole, including our approach for achieving these aims.

Notes

[1] Figures based on people with below average household incomes after housing costs (AHC). Child poverty rates are higher according to official measures (29% in the UK and 30% in Wales).

[2] It has been generally accepted – in UK official statistics and in many countries internationally – that the threshold below which someone is deemed to be of 'low income' is 60% of the median. 'Relative low income' refers to the level of a person's income in comparison to the median of the current year.

This stands in contrast to 'absolute low income', which compares a person's income to the median of the 2010/11 year – a generally accepted benchmark year which allows more easily for comparisons of low income levels over time. The figure stated here relates to official statistics on relative low incomes for 2015–16 (Department for Work and Pensions, 2016).

[3] Problems with the introduction of Universal Credit have been outlined by the Work and Pensions Committee inquiry (House of Commons Work and Pensions Select Committee, 2017). In the news media, the human and administrative costs associated with number of successfully appealed assessments for PIP and ESA have been identified as indicative of systemic problems with those benefits. See, for example, Press Association (2018).

[4] Slightly different methods of calculation are used in England, as figures are considered less sensitive to changes in fuel prices.

[5] Persistent poverty according to the ONS refers to experiencing 'relative low income in the current year, as well as at least 2 out of the 3 preceding years'.

[6] Although Welsh Government tax raising will expand in 2018/19 with new powers to collect tax on land transactions and waste disposal to landfill from April 2018 and partial controls over income tax (for 10p in the pound) from April 2019. https://www.gov.uk/government/news/uk-and-welsh-governments-confirm-next-steps-in-welsh-tax-devolution.

CHAPTER 2

Methodology

This chapter provides an explanation of the approach and method of the empirical research informing this book. Our primary aims in conducting the research have been to produce an evidence base demonstrating how poverty is represented in the news media in Wales, and to explore how and why poverty coverage is produced in the way that it is. The study has been designed and carried out bilingually, in English and in Welsh, in order to address these questions comprehensively and as they are actually played out in the bilingual media environment of Wales. Our focus has been exploring journalistic and editorial practices, including relationships between media and third sector organisations working on poverty issues, and the communications strategies and practices of those organisations and their experiences of engaging with news media in Wales. An additional objective in this is to highlight opportunities and challenges for both news media and the third sector in the reporting of poverty, considering areas of productive exchange as well as lines of tension and sensitivity, which may open up possibilities for changing practice in ways that benefit news narratives on poverty.

Two main methods of data collection have been employed in the study:

1) A content study, involving a systematic quantitative content analysis to explore, in depth, news media coverage of poverty in the English and Welsh languages in Wales.

2) A production study, involving semi-structured interviews to explore the professional practices, experiences and beliefs about poverty and poverty coverage in Wales amongst two key groups:

   a. News media professionals (journalists and editors) working in the English and Welsh languages across broadcast, print and online media whose work involves reporting on poverty in Wales.

   b. Third sector professionals working in the English and Welsh languages across a range of organisations addressing poverty issues

How to cite this book chapter:
Moore, K. 2020. *Reporting on Poverty: News Media Narratives and Third Sector Communications in Wales.* Pp. 11–18. Cardiff: Cardiff University Press. DOI: https://doi.org/10.18573/book4.b. License: CC-BY-NC-ND 4.0

in Wales whose role entails communicating with news media on poverty/poverty-related issues.

The study has been designed in the understanding that the definition of poverty is, in itself, contentious, and we have used these competing definitions to inform our expectations about how poverty *could be* understood and defined by news media. As such, our operational definitions (for the purposes of collecting relevant data in the content study and for providing the focus of discussion in the interviews) are reasonably broad, including any story where 'poverty', low incomes, economic deprivation or insecurity, or social exclusion related to financial hardship were mentioned – either explicitly or implied. In addition, any discussion of causes, impact or consequences of poverty was included in the study. This has allowed us to comprehensively capture coverage of the key issue stake culturally, socially and politically in the reproduction of the dominant 'discourses', or ideas commonly associated with poverty, in our content study. It has also allowed us to explore a range of relevant experiences and perspectives on poverty and poverty news and media communications in our interviews. Paying attention to these ideas as they are expressed in the language of the news and in the practices of news making matters, not only because they may involve fair or unfair, inaccurate or inaccurate representations of people experiencing poverty but because these representations 'frame' poverty – they are what make poverty meaningful – contributing to popular understandings of what poverty *is*, *why* it exists and *how* it should be dealt with. In other words, the ideas circulating in news contribute to the construction and reproduction of the practical or concrete social realities of poverty and its social, political and institutional management.

The news media content analysis

For eight weeks between 4 April and 15 July 2016 (40 days in total), the news media in Wales was intensively monitored for all coverage relating to poverty. The sample included English- and Welsh-language daily and weekly newspapers, television and radio news, and online news in English. The period of monitoring extended from 4 April to 15 July 2016, with alternate weeks selected to capture a breadth of coverage across this period as well as any major stories continuing for longer than one day.[1] The media selected included that produced by both commercial and public media organisations, targeted at a range of different audiences in Wales, and with significant circulation figures/reach as set out in Table 1 below. In total, 60 hours of television news and 80 hours of radio news were reviewed. These were largely accessed through the 'Box of Broadcasts' archive (BOB), although researchers also visited BBC Wales and ITV Wales archives to access material unavailable through BOB due to technical glitches. The Nexis database of newspapers was used to obtain the majority of the print news sample, although back copies of two weekly titles – the *Carmarthen Journal* and *Golwg* were obtained in hard copy.

Table 1: Media included in content analysis sample.

Print	Television	Radio	Online
Western Mail Publisher: Trinity Location: Cardiff Reach: 19,910 daily Language: English	BBC Wales Today 18.30–19.00	BBC Radio Cymru: Post Cyntaf 7.05–8.05	Wales Online Publisher: Media Wales Location: Cardiff Language: English
South Wales Argus Publisher: Newsquest Location: Newport Reach: 13,000 daily Language: English	ITV Wales Tonight 18.00–13.30	BBC Radio Wales: Good Morning Wales 7.05–8.05	
Daily Post Publisher: Trinity Location: Llundudno Reach: 25,426 daily Language: English	S4C Newyddion 9 21.00–21.30		
Camarthen Journal Publisher: Trinity Location: Camarthen Reach: 12,400 weekly Language: English			
Golwg Publisher: WAG/Welsh Book Council Reach: 2,500–3,000 weekly Language: Welsh			

A bespoke tool using Python PI to search and scrape relevant content from online news was developed by Cardiff University computational journalism and computer science colleagues Glynn Mottershead and Martin Chorley, and this was used to capture our sample of news from Wales Online.

All coverage explicitly relating to poverty, economic inequality, disadvantage or marginalisation in the UK was included in the sample analysed. This involved stories focused directly on poverty as a 'main theme' as well as those in which its mention was more incidental. An extensive keyword list was piloted and refined and used to inform database searches. In addition, a manual filtering process to remove any irrelevant material picked up was used. An equivalent list translated into Welsh was used for searches of Welsh-language media (keyword lists are included in Appendix A). Comprehensive piloting to ensure consistency in story relevance decisions across media types was conducted, and monitoring continued throughout the study using a 'coding manual' as a reference document for coding decisions. This meant that different coders could, over a prolonged period, conduct analyses consistently, distinguishing between articles to be included in our sample and those to be excluded, as well as finer coding decisions. For example, articles which covered unemployment were included in the sample, but articles that focused on the national economy or business generally, which discussed the fortunes of the state or of companies but which made no manifest reference to economic impacts upon individuals, groups or communities (such as job insecurity or redundancies) were excluded.

In all, 1,498 news items in total were coded. A breakdown of the sample by media type and language medium is provided in Table 2 below.

Each of the 1,498 news items was coded according to a number of measures designed to explore how poverty and those affected by it in various ways have been identified and represented in the news media. These included:

- The main themes of stories and issues most frequently associated with poverty.
- The individuals and groups identified as experiencing poverty.
- How poverty is contextualised, including the geographical areas in which reports were situated.
- How poverty is framed in reporting: the reasons outlined for poverty, any attribution of responsibility or solutions suggested and any consequences of poverty mentioned.
- Who has a voice in poverty coverage (the individuals or organisations used by journalists as sources) and the gender, if applicable, of those voices.

Table 2: Number of news items by media type.

	TV		Radio		Print		Online		Totals
English language	BBC Wales	89	Good Morning Wales	140	Western Mail	198	Wales Online	528	
	ITV Wales	69			Daily Post	82			
					South Wales Argus	63			
					Carmarthen Journal	46			1215
Welsh language	S4C	112	Post Cyntaf	146	Golwg	25			283
Total		270		286		414		528	1498

The full coding scheme for the content study is included in the appendices (included at the end of the book). The resulting data was entered into a statistical software package (SPSS) in order to produce detailed frequency and cross tabulation findings, and these are presented in Chapter 3.

The production study: interviews with journalists and third sector professionals

Between the summers of 2016 and 2017 a series of semi-structured interviews was conducted with 19 journalists and editors whose work had involved reporting on poverty issues, drawn from news and current affairs on television, radio, online and print in the Welsh and English languages in Wales. A parallel series of semi-structured interviews was also conducted with 16 professionals working in third sector organisations whose roles have involved communicating with news and/or current affairs media. Interviews lasted between one and two hours and were conducted in either English or Welsh (according to the interviewee's preference). Interviews were predominantly conducted face to face, either in participants' workplaces or at Cardiff University. Several interviews were conducted either via Skype or by telephone. All participants were fully briefed about the aims of the project and the purpose of their potential participation in the research and written consent obtained from all participants.[2] Although most journalists and editors were happy to be identified, all interview research data collected has been anonymised in the write-up of this study to ensure confidentiality, as far as possible, to all participants. One of the particular ethical concerns of the research team related to the possible inadvertent disclosure of participant identities through the networking and impact activities associated with the project. The potential for inference of identity from attendance at workshops or meetings, and/or conversations held at the event held in April 2017 in Cardiff, was set out clearly as part of the consent process. In addition, the potential of identification from turn of phrase in interview responses or from references to particular experiences in reporting or communications activities due to the 'small world' environment of media and communications in Wales was also highlighted to participants.

The interviews with news media professionals were designed with to explore a number of issues, including:

- Current journalistic expectations or understandings about the stories to be told about poverty and poverty-related issues in Wales.
- How institutional roles, responsibilities and constraints in journalism might influence the coverage output on poverty.
- Everyday newsroom routines and experiences of reporting poverty-related issues.

- Journalists' understandings of news values, how these might affect poverty coverage and the role journalism plays in shaping ideas about poverty in Wales.
- People or organisations understood to be ideal/valuable sources or perspectives in reporting poverty issues and impediments to accessing sources whom journalists would like to access more regularly.
- Relationships between journalists working in Wales and the third sector.

The design of interviews with third sector professionals included a range of issues designed to mirror and intersect with those covered with journalists in order to provide a coherent picture of the similarities and tensions between the two groups with respect to representing poverty narratives in Wales. These issues included:

- How third sector professionals seek to represent the voices and stories of those they support in their communications practices.
- How the institutional roles, responsibilities and other pressures may influence communications practices.
- Understandings of the role journalism plays in shaping ideas about poverty in Wales.
- Understandings of news values, how journalists report on poverty and perceptions of the current news narrative on poverty.
- How, if at all, third sector professionals seek to influence news narratives and to what degree of success.
- Beliefs about newsworthy stories that are not being told and potential (re) sources for news that journalists do not currently access.
- Relationships between third sector professionals and the news media in Wales.[3]

All interviews were audio-recorded and transcribed, with translation into English for all interviews conducted in Welsh. A systematic thematic analysis of each interview corpus was carried out, aided by a coding process conducted using the computer software program NVivo. These analyses are presented in Chapter 4 and Chapter 5 of this book.[4]

An ongoing conversation with industry professionals: Exploring the Narrative workshop, networking and training events

In April 2017 a set of workshops and a networking evening event was held in Cardiff, which highlighted a clear common interest in generating impact from the research.[5] The event was attended by 11 different third sector organisations, including homelessness charities, housing associations, advice and advocacy organisations and NGOs. Representatives from the news media working

Hidden poverty is on the rise; so if it's harder to see, is it harder to report?

Today nearly one in four people in Wales live in poverty. A combination of cuts, rising costs and poor quality jobs mean that more and more of us are trying to keep the wolf from the door. Yet poverty is not always easy to see. You can have a smartphone but no money to feed your family. You can be holding down a job but sofa surfing. You can be smartly dressed but riddled with worry and debt.

What is the media's role in reporting this poverty accurately? How can reporters find individuals who are willing to share their stories in today's digital world, which opens the door to judgement and abuse? What safeguarding measures should the media take when working with vulnerable people? And what role do charities and anti-poverty organisations play in getting individual stories out there to raise awareness of the wider problem?

Reporting on Poverty will tackle these challenging questions head on, hear directly from people with lived experience of poverty who have worked with the media, and provide a space for frank and honest discussion. It will be an invaluable opportunity for journalists, media organisations, public bodies and the Welsh third sector.

#Reportingonpoverty

Mae tlodi cudd ar gynnydd; felly os yw'n anos ei weld, a yw'n anos gohebu arno?

Heddiw, mae bron i un ym mhob pedwar o bobl yng Nghymru yn byw mewn tlodi. Mae cyfuniad o doriadau, costau cynyddol a swyddi ansawdd gwael yn golygu bod mwy a mwy ohonom yn ceisio cadw'r blaidd rhag y drws. Ond nid yw tlodi'n hawdd ei weld bob amser. Mae'n bosib i rywun fod â ffôn clyfar ond ddim arian i fwydo ei deulu. Mae'n bosib i rywun fod â swydd ond yn cysgu ar soffa yn nhŷ rhywun arall. Mae'n bosib i rywun fod wedi gwisgo'n smart ond yn llawn gofid ac mewn dyledion mawr.

Beth yw rôl y cyfryngau wrth ohebu'n gywir ar y tlodi hwn? Sut y gall gohebwyr ddod o hyd i unigolion sy'n fodlon rhannu eu straeon yn y byd digidol sydd ohoni, sy'n agor y drws i feirniadaeth a sarhad? Pa fesurau diogelwch y dylai'r cyfryngau eu cymryd wrth weithio gyda phobl fregus? A pha rôl y mae elusennau a sefydliadau gwrthdlodi yn ei chwarae o ran rhannu straeon unigolion er mwyn codi ymwybyddiaeth o'r broblem ehangach?

Bydd Gohebu ar Dlodi yn mynd i'r afael â'r cwestiynau heriol hyn, yn gyfle i glywed yn uniongyrchol gan bobl sydd wedi cael profiad o dlodi eu hunain ac wedi gweithio gyda'r cyfryngau, ac yn cynnig llwyfan ar gyfer trafodaeth onest ac agored. Bydd yn gyfle amhrisiadwy i newyddiadurwyr, sefydliadau'r cyfryngau, cyrff cyhoeddus a'r trydydd sector yng Nghymru.

##AdroddArDlodi

Figure 1: Brief for 'Reporting on Poverty' event, 8 November 2018.

in print, broadcast and online journalism in Wales, as well as a journalist and editor working in national broadcast news, also attended. The event provided an opportunity to share and invite reflections upon preliminary findings from the content study and to discuss and invite feedback on issues emerging from the interview data. It functioned to involve key stakeholders in the interpretation of the research and to begin to explore how the research could be used to facilitate and support improved networks of understanding, communication and working relationships between organisations working in the third sector on poverty issues and journalists reporting on these issues in Wales.

In November 2018, we followed up this work with a bilingual training event aimed primarily at journalists, 'Reporting on Poverty', which was organised jointly with the National Union of Journalists Training Wales and Oxfam Cymru. The main aims of this event were to encourage industry professionals (including journalists working in print news and across the main public and commercial broadcasters, as well as freelance journalists) to critically reflect upon experiences of poverty reporting in the interests of 'best practice', drawing upon the implications of key findings from the 'Exploring the Narrative' research. The event engaged with 'experiences' of poverty reporting from several perspectives, including those of journalists and editors working in national UK and Wales-based media, those of communications professionals in NGOs, and those of ordinary people who had previously told their stories to the media. In response to some of the key findings of this research, a large part of the day's discussion was 'case studies', and the challenges of rendering reporting meaningful and relevant to audiences through the incorporation of 'real-life' examples and human interest angles whilst reporting people's stories fairly, sensitively and ethically. With the launch and ongoing discussion of this book, our hope is to further build upon these engagement activities with industry professionals, and to further these processes of reflection on reporting poverty practices.

Notes

[1] Selected media monitoring periods: Period 1: 4 April–8 April; Period 2: 18 April–22 April; Period 3: 2 May–6 May; Period 4: 16 May–20 May; Period 5: 30 May–3 June; Period 6: 13 June–17 June; Period 7: 27 June–1 July; Period 8: 11 July–15 July.

[2] Example information sheets and consent materials for each group are included as Appendices D and E.

[3] The broad schedules of questions from which interviews were conducted with each group of professionals are included in Appendix F.

[4] Preliminary reflections and feedback on some of the interview material, focusing on issues surrounding case studies in reporting, were solicited from third sector professionals who attended the workshops held in Cardiff in April 2017.

[5] This work, 'Using Research Findings about the Media Narrative on Poverty in Wales to Build Journalist–Third Sector Communications Networks', was facilitated by ESRC Impact Acceleration funding.

CHAPTER 3

Findings of the Content Analysis Study

Introduction

The spring and summer of 2016 brought three major news stories carrying considerable significance for media audiences in Wales as well as for the UK as a whole. Our monitoring of coverage relating to poverty from 4 April to 15 July captured 1,498 news items including, as Figure 1 shows, the Tata Steel crisis in Port Talbot in April, the Welsh Assembly Government Elections on 5 May and the referendum on Britain's membership of the European Union on 23 June.

In addition, this period featured the reporting of numerous other business crises posing threats to jobs, the prosperity of local communities and the wider economy. These included uncertainties surrounding the future of the major 'Circuit of Wales' infrastructure project in Ebbw Vale, job cuts at Airbus and the Dow Corning chemical plant in Barry, a planned restructuring at Sainsbury's and several other retail chains, including convenience store 'My Local' and high street retailers BHS and Austin Reed, going into administration.

The relevance of poverty-related issues emanating from these events and others could be traced in much of the politically focused coverage. For example, the challenge to Jeremy Corbyn's leadership of the Labour Party prior to his re-election in September 2016 elicited reporting that profiled Labour positions and priorities and which discussed issues such as opposing austerity politics, protecting jobs and those most vulnerable to government cuts and the uncertain economic climate surrounding Brexit. Similarly, MP Stephen Crabb's bid for the Conservative Party leadership, announced in June 2016, profiled his working-class upbringing on a council estate in Pembrokeshire and 'blue collar conservatism' candidacy.

We also saw stories at a more local, civic or personal level – telling the story of people's experiences of business crises and the sharp day-to-day human realities of government cuts, including job and/or pension insecurity, vulnerability to debt, the struggle to pay bills and vulnerability to homelessness or of homeless people. Some

How to cite this book chapter:
Moore, K. 2020. *Reporting on Poverty: News Media Narratives and Third Sector Communications in Wales.* Pp. 19–51. Cardiff: Cardiff University Press. DOI: https://doi.org/10.18573/book4.c. License: CC-BY-NC-ND 4.0

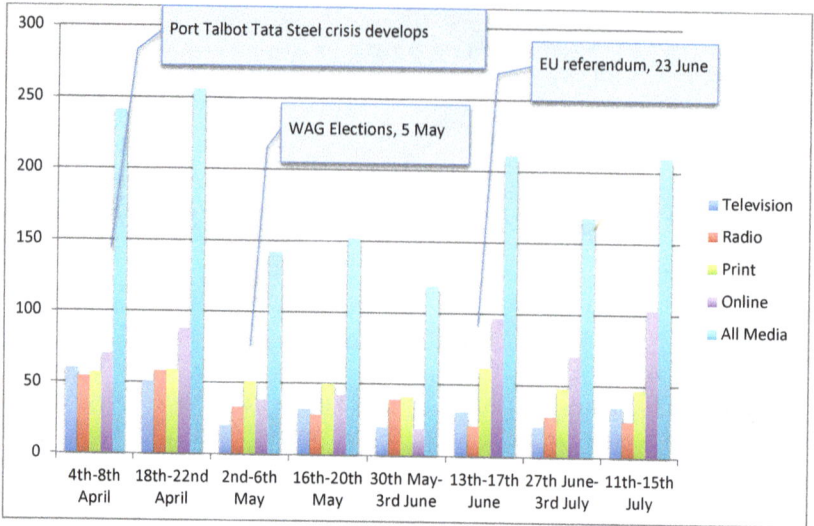

Figure 2: Volume and timeline of coverage.

coverage also focused on law and order, featuring the personal costs of becoming the victim of fraud or other crime depriving them of essential income or assets, as well as an extraordinary case involving forced labour and modern slavery.

In this chapter we set out in detail the key findings of our systematic, quantitative study of the content of the media in Wales during this period. It is set out to enable comparison of poverty coverage by media type, focusing on broad patterns in the volume and characteristics of reporting, identifying similarities and differences in the thematic focus, contextualising details and framing features represented. Some of the key stories underpinning this data are also explored more qualitatively to contextualise these comparisons and to demonstrate something further about how those stories were represented, and especially how ideas and emotions surrounding precarious livelihoods featured in the news.

Groups and locations featured

We examined which groups, if any, were explicitly identified as experiencing or affected by poverty. In all, 2,148 mentions of groups were included across the 1,498 news items analysed. The largest category of person identified was 'workers' (in 41% of news items, n=614), followed by references to 'the community' or the public in general (28% of news items, n=420).

References to demographic groups identified by more specific detail were less common, and made up a much lower proportion of all mentions of groups experiencing poverty, for example youth (18.8%, n=282), parents and families (9.1%, n=136), the elderly (6.5%, n=98), people with a disability (4.3% of news items), refugees (2.3%), others with a migrant background (1.4% of news

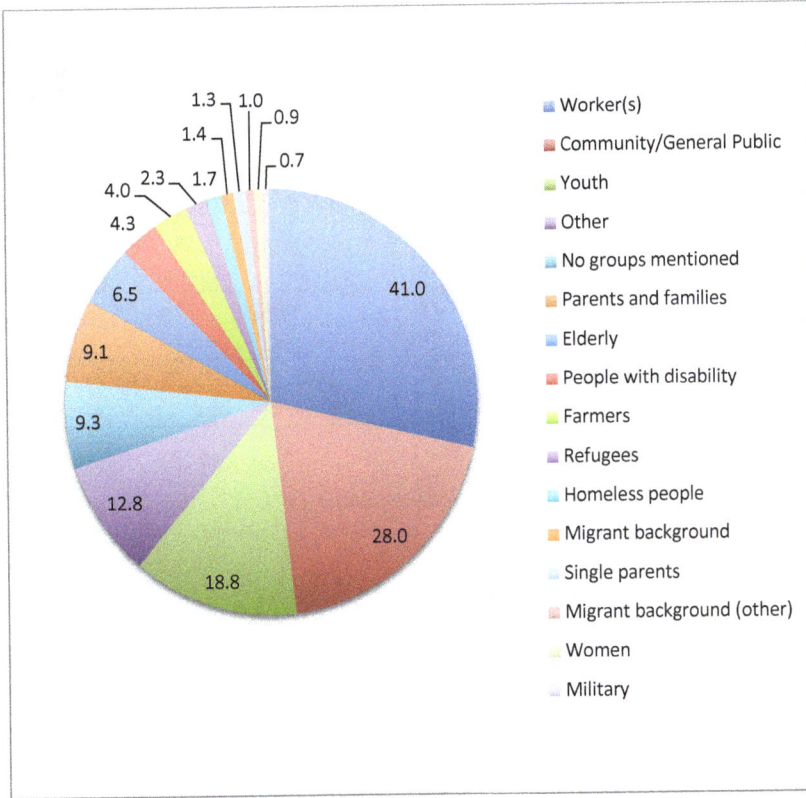

Figure 3: Groups affected by poverty featured across coverage (n=1498).

Table 3: Geographical location of news coverage (as % of news items).

	TV	Radio	Print	Online	All media
Other city/ town/region	46.3% (n=125)	34.3% (n=98)	40.1% (n=166)	32.4% (n=171)	37.4% (n=560)
Wales in general	39.3% (n=106)	36% (n=103)	33.6% (n=139)	33.3% (n=176)	35% (n=524)
UK in general	11.1% (n=30)	25.2% (n=72)	27.8% (n=115)	22.2% (n=117)	22.3% (n=334)
Port Talbot	11.5% (n=31)	6.6% (n=19)	10.4% (n=43)	10.2% (n=54)	9.8% (n=147)
'The Valleys'	9.6% (n=26)	4.5% (n=13)	2.7% (n=11)	15% (n=79)	8.6% (n=129)
Cardiff	6.7% (n=18)	2.4% (n=7)	2.9% (n=12)	14% (n=74)	7.4% (n=111)

contd.

Table 3: *contd.*

	TV	Radio	Print	Online	All media
International	2.2% (n=6)	10.8% (n=31)	7.5% (n=31)	4.5% (n=24)	6.1% (n=92)
Elsewhere in UK	1.5% (n=4)	1.0% (n=3)	2.9% (n=12)	2.8% (n=15)	2.3% (n=34)
Swansea	1.5% (n=4)	1.4% (n=4)	1.9% (n=8)	2.7% (n=14)	2% (n=30)
Other	1.1% (n=3)	0% (n=0)	0.2% (n=1)	0.2% (n=1)	0.3% (n=5)
All mentions	130.7% (n=353)	122.4% (n=350)	130% (n=538)	137.3% (n=725)	131.2% (n=1966)

items), single parents (1.3%, n=20) or women (0.9%, n=11). In 9.3% (n=140) of news items in our sample, although issues related to poverty were discussed, no specific group was identified as affected. However, it should be emphasised that these results do not mean that readers might not infer from the issues covered that certain groups could be affected in some way, but rather that reports did not *explicitly* feature or refer to those lived effects. So, for example, although the issue of economic deprivation may have featured in a report discussing the state of the economy, any tangible sense of how these issues may have been experienced in the lives of people may not.

In order to identify whether coverage focused on some geographical areas more regularly than others in news featuring poverty, we also analysed where stories were located. In many articles, more than one location was mentioned, e.g. a story might comment upon employment insecurity in the UK in general, and then focus upon experiences of unemployment in a particular town in Wales (hence all mentions in each media type total more than 100%). The coverage across media types was reasonably diverse in terms of the geographical location of coverage, with the largest category overall 'other city/town/region' (37.4% of news items, n=560). These included other specific mentions of locations in Wales such as Ebbw Vale, Newport and a mixture of small and large towns in West and North Wales. The next most significant category represented was 'Wales in general' (35%, n=524).

Port Talbot steel workers' crisis

Our data reflects how news coverage during this period connected concerns about poverty and livelihoods under threat with the problems workers were facing in many areas of Wales as big employers based in those areas experienced difficulties. Featuring largest amongst these was the Tata Steel plant in Port

Talbot, and, as such, the social actors whose experiences most often featured were workers, who due to the demographic profile of that group were generally featured as male. Although some reporting did focus on more specific social groups, in large parts of the coverage the social profile of people at the sharp end of destabilising employment situations often did not feature strongly. Instead, references to the likelihood that communities that would 'suffer' as a result of businesses collapsing or the steel industry crisis were common.

For example, In a live blog piece detailing events as they unfolded on 'Welsh Steel in Crisis', including a debate in the Welsh Assembly: 'Carwyn Jones Stands "Shoulder to Shoulder" with Steelworkers – and List of Potential Buyers Grows – Recap' (Wales Online, 4 April 2016), Carwyn Jones's statement is featured as a 'Key Event':

> 13.47: 'We stand beside you shoulder to shoulder' AMs bang their desks as Carwyn Jones says the Assembly will stand alongside steelworkers. 'The workforce, communities and families are at the heart of what must be done, but seeking a solution has nothing to do with sentiment. The UK needs a steel industry,' he said. He says the UK Government should nationalise the plants if it needs to keep them going until a buyer is found. And he finishes by saying we stand beside the steel communities shoulder to shoulder.

The expression of solidarity in this political discourse resonates as it evokes the spectre of pain and loss, socially, politically and economically, associated with historic deindustrialisation for communities in Wales. In news items focusing more closely on the experiences of those communities in relation to steelworkers' jobs and pensions, solidarity and multiple references to past industrial closures and job losses also figure large. For example, in a detailed piece, 'How Steelworkers' Pensions Look Set to Suffer under Any Deal to Save Port Talbot', the potential fate of workers' pensions is outlined with reference to the 2002 collapse of Cardiff steelmaker Allied Steel and Wire (ASW). The article focuses firmly on workers' interests, including ASW workers' perspectives on the significant personal losses previously experienced (and now at stake) should the Tata workers' only recourse turn out be the Pensions Protection Fund (PPF):

> We will still fight for our pensions to be fully restored, and if Tata workers enter the PPF we will fight for them, Unlike politicians who are telling the country we are all in this together, steelworkers will stick together. (Wales Online, 5 May)

Several emotionally expressive Wales Online pieces sought to bring the voices of affected workers and their communities, past and present, to the fore. In 'Heavy Metal and Steel: Ebbw Vale Festival to Remember Closed Works as Port

Talbot Crisis Deepens' (Wales Online, 8 April), an upcoming festival about steel in South Wales valleys town Ebbw Vale is profiled. The voices of event organisers are cited, setting fears and anxieties surrounding Port Talbot's future are set in context of the historic decline of the industry in the area:

> I'd rather this event wasn't given such stark relevance by the prospect of more steelworkers and their families facing an uncertain future, but the unbearable prospect faced by the Port Talbot community actually happened here in Ebbw Vale.

In an especially poignant piece trailing a Channel 4 news item about a street of residents whose lives and livelihoods over several generations have been bound to the steelworks, 'How One Street in the Shadow of Port Talbot's Steelworks is Facing the Future' (Wales Online, 12 July), Darren Devine writes that it 'captures the life of the community under threat':

> Children play on bikes while neighbours sit outside the row of terraced houses chatting. It could be any terraced street in any Welsh industrial heartland. But the threat posed by the remote Indian conglomerate sets it apart … They live just a stone's throw from the works that has provided jobs and prosperity for decades.
>
> But for seven months they have lived with the knowledge the certainties their lives have been built on could crumble.

Similarly, the feature article 'Three Generations of This Family Are All Proud to Say They Have Worked in Port Talbot's Steel Industry' (Wales Online, 15 April) offered an extended reflection upon the experiences of workers at Port Talbot, examining the aspirations and expectations of several generations of residents that the plant would provide secure employment and comfortable livelihoods, as well as personal experiences of changing workplace cultures and the political-economies of steel over the decades. An especially memorable article conveying these narratives appeared in the *Western Mail* (8 April): 'Little Girl's Post Plea to Save Her Father's Job'. Emotively, the child, Neve, appeals to politicians to act to avert the loss – not only of her father's job but her own future and the town's very vitality:

> I am scared that if the steelworks closes this town will be worse than it is now. We have all charity shops and we need to make sure people have other jobs to go to. I wanted to grow up and live in Port Talbot but now I think there's nothing here, which makes me sad.

Through the intimate, cross-generational story of political protest of this article, the threatened livelihoods of Port Talbot families are powerfully represented through a subjunctive appeal to what ought to be – an alternative vision of opportunity, security and aspiration, set against a stark image of symbolic urban emptiness, commercial abandonment and future decline.

Whilst a significant proportion of our sample's coverage was comprised of articles focused upon official political discourse and/or that analysed the business or economic dynamics of the steel crisis at much more of a distance, it's important to also highlight these more human stories, where the political and emotional imaginary attendant to historical narratives of industrial decline played a central role. Whether very much laid bare (as in Neve's plea) or more condensed (as in Carwyn Jones's loaded political message, live blogged in the Welsh Assembly debate), the will to secure attention to the very real human experiences of the steel crisis, and not just the economic and political dynamics of its unfolding, was very evident in this section of the coverage.

Main themes and 'news hooks'

As set out in our methodology chapter, our sample includes all news items featuring poverty, economic inequality or social marginalisation. However, whilst some news reports afford centrality to these issues, others feature them as more marginal aspects of the story. Table 4 sets out the poverty-related issues identified as a main theme, and those where they were mentioned otherwise, as part of a report focused more on other issues.

Poverty-related issues were a main theme in just over a third of the coverage analysed (34%, n=525). They were more likely to be represented as a main theme in print news articles (41.1%, n=170) than in any of the other news media, and least likely in television coverage (28.9%, n=78), although, due to variations in the total number of news items across media type within the sample, there were more main theme news items online (n=177) than in any other media.

In order to provide a more detailed context for how poverty-related issues appeared within news coverage, the 'main theme' of all articles was coded.

Table 4: Poverty-related issue as main/other theme (as % of news items).

	Television	Radio	Print	Online	Total
Main theme	28.9% (n=78)	35% (n=100)	41.1% (n=170)	33.5% (n=177)	35% (n=525)
Other	71.1% (n=192)	65% (n=186)	58.9% (n=244)	66.5% (n=351)	65% (n=973)
Total	100% (n=270)	100% (n=286)	100% (n=414)	100% (n=528)	100% (n=1498)

As Table 5 below shows, across different news types, the coverage was domi-
nated by the themes of the economy (35.9% of news items, n=538) and politics (29.6% of news items, n=444). With significantly less frequency, a range of
other themes was identified in the coverage, with some variation across news
types. For example, whilst 'law and order' (10.6%, n=44) was the next most

Table 5: Main theme of news items (as % of news items).

	Television	Radio	Print	Online	All media
Economy	40.7% (n=110)	40.6% (n=116)	30.4% (n=126)	35.2% (n=186)	35.9% (n=538)
Politics	32.6% (n=88)	25.9% (n=74)	32.4% (n=134)	28% (n=148)	29.6% (n=444)
Health	4.8% (n=13)	6.3% (n=18)	7% (n=29)	8% (n=42)	6.8% (n=102)
Law/order	4.4% (n=12)	3.8% (n=11)	10.6% (n=44)	6.1% (n=32)	6.6% (n=99)
Education	8.5% (n=23)	9.1% (n=26)	2.4% (n=10)	6.3% (n=33)	6.1% (n=92)
Charity (other)	2.2% (n=6)	3.1% (n=9)	9.9% (n=41)	6.4% (n=34)	6% (n=90)
Other	2.6% (n=7)	0.7% (n=2)	1.9% (n=8)	3.8% (n=20)	2.5% (n=37)
Sport/recreation	1.1% (n=3)	1% (n=3)	1.7% (n=7)	4% (n=21)	2.3% (n=34)
Migration	1.1% (n=3)	2.1% (n=6)	1% (n=4)	1.3% (n=7)	1.3% (n=20)
International aid	0.4% (n=1)	2.4% (n=7)	1.7% (n=7)	0% (n=0)	1% (n=15)
Europe	0.4% (n=1)	1.7% (n=5)	0.5% (n=2)	0.4% (n=2)	0.7% (n=10)
Foreign policy/ affairs other	0.4% (n=2)	2.4% (n=7)	0.2% (n=1)	0% (n=0)	0.7% (n=10)
Security	0.4% (n=1)	0.7% (n=2)	0% (n=0)	0.2% (n=1)	0.3% (n=4)
Local government	0% (n=0)	0% (n=0)	0.2% (n=1)	0.2% (n=1)	0.1% (n=2)
Religion	0% (n=0)	0% (n=0)	0% (n=0)	0.2% (n=1)	0.1% (n=1)
Total	100% (n=270)	100% (n=286)	100% (n=414)	100% (n=528)	100% (n=1498)

significant theme in print, in broadcast news it was 'education' – featuring in 9.1% (n=26) of radio items and 8.5% (n=23) of television items, and 'health' was the next most important theme online (8%, n=42).

To further demonstrate the context or framing of poverty-related issues in the coverage, we also analysed the 'news hooks'. Although related to 'themes', this variable more specifically addressed the main generative cause or reason it seemed that a news story had appeared.

The news hook data provides a more nuanced insight into the routes through which poverty, economic inequality and social marginalisation issues made it into news agendas during our period of monitoring. It is perhaps unsurprising given the major news events during this time that the top three news hooks across the coverage were 'WAG report/policy/politics' (22.6%, n=268), business

Table 6: News hooks (as % of news items).

News hook	Television	Radio	Print	Online	All media
WAG report/ policy/politics	33% (n=89)	29.7% (n=85)	16.4% (n=68)	18.2% (n=96)	22.6% (n=338)
Business activity	17.4% (n=47)	17.5% (n=50)	15.2% (n=63)	20.5% (n=108)	17.9% (n=268)
EU referendum	15.6% (n=42)	16.1% (n=46)	16.7% (n=69)	17.4% (n=92)	16.6% (n=249)
UK national government report/ policy/politics	7.4% (n=20)	14% (n=40)	12.6% (n=52)	10.6% (n=56)	11.2% (n=168)
Charity/third sector activity	6.3% (n=17)	9.4% (n=27)	14.7% (n=61)	9.3% (n=49)	10.3% (n=154)
Local authority/ council report/ policy/politics	5.2% (n=14)	4.2% (n=12)	5.6% (n=23)	6.3% (n=33)	5.5% (n=82)
Experiences of poverty	2.2% (n=6)	2.8% (n=8)	3.9% (n=16)	7.8% (n=41)	4.7% (n=71)
Law and order	3.3% (n=9)	0.3% (n=1)	8.7% (n=36)	3.6% (n=19)	4.3% (n=65)
Other	3.7% (n=10)	3.5% (n=10)	2.9% (n=12)	4.5% (n=24)	3.7% (n=56)
Strike or union protest	5.2% (n=14)	2.1% (n=6)	2.9% (n=12)	1.1% (n=6)	2.5% (n=38)
Opinion poll	0.7% (n=2)	0.3% (n=1)	0.5% (n=2)	0.8% (n=4)	0.6% (n=9)
Total	100% (n=270)	100% (n=286)	100% (n=414)	100% (n=528)	100% (n=1498)

activity (17.9% of news items, n=268) and the EU referendum (16.6%, n=249). There were some variations between news types, however, with the most important print news hooks focused on the EU referendum (16.7%, n=69), whilst online news hooks were most likely to be focused on business activity (20.5%, n=108).

EU referendum coverage

When we look more closely at the EU referendum coverage captured within our sample, we see that the main themes of most stories (perhaps unsurprisingly) were either politics (n=135) or economics (n=94). Amongst this coverage were claims that leaving, or that remaining in the EU, would lead to more poverty in Wales. Very often, unless an article was a comment piece from a spokesperson from one or other camps, both leave and remain voices were included within a single news item, to convey a sense of journalistic objectivity, especially in the weeks preceding the vote. The coverage also profiled people's hopes and fears about the expected economic consequences of the decision by both camps during the campaign, and especially in its immediate aftermath.

In the run-up to the vote, some coverage dealt in with the anticipated impact of Brexit on businesses, specific industries and the economy more generally in Wales. For example, in 'Brexit Will Send Farming Back to Depression Years', for example, Farmer's Union of Wales (FUW) president Glyn Roberts's position that 'failure to reform UK agricultural policy, in the event of an Out vote, would "decimate Welsh farming" and leave rural areas "facing levels of poverty not seen since the 1930s"' frames the discussion in the subjunctive with an appeal to recognise what could be at stake, socio-economically, for Wales should politicians fail to recognise the interests of the agricultural industry (*Daily Post*, 16 June). Similarly, in 'The Great Divide: Remain and Create Jobs or Leave and Strip Away Red Tape' (*Daily Post*, 15 June), although Leave campaign claims about the potential advantages of Brexit for small and medium enterprises (SMEs) bidding for public sector contracts are included, these are set against a raft of official sources academic expertise and industry groups arguing for the economic benefits of remaining. Quoted at length, Tracy North, North Wales chair of the Confederation of British Industry (CBI), sets out a clear rationale, linked tangibly to jobs and livelihoods informing these positions:

> The sheer weight of credible economic evidence, including from the Government, the IMF and the London School of Economics, makes it crystal clear that there would be a serious shock to the UK economy should we leave the EU. Being inside the EU has provided huge trade and investment benefits to ambitious Welsh firms – small, medium and large – over the last 40 years, helping to create jobs and raise living standards in this country. This is why the mainstream business view and that of the majority of CBI member companies is to stay in the EU.

The alternatives to membership leave us on the outside, following rules without any say in how they are set, and in many cases still footing the bill. Those advocating an exit from the EU need to spell out exactly how the UK will be better off.

Indeed, in much of the coverage a more substantive set of economic arguments, apparently underpinned by expertise or support from official institutions from the Remain camp, are set against a raft of seemingly more hypothetical or hopeful claims from the Leave campaign. The latter, often communicated through the voices of 'ordinary people', also articulated EU membership with an array of observable discontents with the status quo and speculation about future troubles, including the economic problems of southern EU member states, the migrant crisis in the Mediterranean, prospective Turkish membership of the EU, and the loss of steel jobs due to imports of Chinese steel. In a 6 April letter to the editor in the *Western Mail*, for example, Dafydd Rees from Tregaron represents these as an equivalent list of EU problems, in opposition to which, he asserts confidently, Wales will be 'better off' by leaving: 'I believe the UK (and Wales) would be far better off as part of a global free trade area and not be subjected to absurd laws, restrictive practices, bureaucracy and ongoing financial demands of the EU.'

Other stories explored specific campaign claims about how EU rules impacted the cost of living and people's bills. For example, in 'Brexit campaigns cheaper energy bills claim "fantasy"' (*Western Mail*, 1 June), the Leave campaign's claims to be defending the interests of the least wealthy are challenged. Although the headline frames the article with a challenge from Remain, the claims themselves feature strongly in the article, alongside other pro-leave opinions. For example, Vote Leave Cymru spokesman's assertion that 'As a country we'll have more money to spend on our priorities, wages will be higher and fuel bills will be lower' is included, repeating the (already challenged) idea that Brexit will address damaging levels of VAT on fuel which are controlled by the EU. Focusing on tourism and complaints about inadequate transport in rural areas, the article includes quotes from wavering voters disgruntled with the status quo alongside extended quotations of avowed leavers, such as Ashford Price, chairman of the Dan-yr-Ogof National Showcaves Centre for Wales. Claiming that leaving would make Wales more attractive to tourists and offer an opportunity for people's voices to be heard, Price asserts:

It will I think make us far more of a place to visit in our own right so, yeah, I'm all for giving it a go … I think if we don't grab this opportunity we are going to regret it in the long run … what I would like to see happen is that there's a massive vote to leave and then the political bureaucracy will start listening to the people again.

Therefore, although the factual veracity of Leave's claims about the positive impact of Brexit on livelihoods is seriously questioned, these claims nonetheless set the terms of the debate to which 'Remain' voices responded.

Indeed, in much of the news coverage, and perhaps the campaign discourse more generally, the problem of how to respond to or otherwise deal with claims that appeared to be unsubstantiated by evidence or expertise seemed to preoccupy debate. For example, In 'Brexit Will "Tighten Household Budgets across All Income Levels" Says Latest Economic Study' (*Western Mail*, 3 June), London School of Economics (LSE) research is reported which 'appears to counter claims by "leave" campaigners that the rich will bear the economic brunt of leaving the EU while the poor will be better off'. Whilst the LSE's research evidence (that Brexit would negatively impact livelihoods at all levels) appears to set the article's agenda, the narrative is nonetheless preoccupied with reclaiming attention for and reasserting the credibility of 'facts' and 'expertise' in the Brexit debate. As such, warnings feature from Remain voices, such as Greg Hands, chief secretary to the Treasury, for example, seeking to redirect attention to experts: 'When highly respected economists warn families would be thousands of pounds worse off if we leave the EU, everyone should sit up and listen. All the experts are clear that leaving Europe would be a disaster for the British economy.'

This issue of how to secure attention for the Remain case was also evident in the publication of an article campaigning for 'Remain': 'Nine reasons why Wales Will Be Better Off if We Vote to Stay in the EU' (Wales Online, 13 June). An extraordinary intervention from editors at Media Wales, publishers of Wales Online and the *Western Mail*, the article unequivocally sets out a case for Wales to remain in the EU and aligns both titles with this position. The issues of poverty and prosperity are positioned at number one on the list:

> The risk to jobs and livelihoods in the next decade is immense. Divorce from the EU will be painful. The uncertainty two years of renegotiation would be devastating in Wales. Overseas employers would not invest here. Exporters would choose to trust their future to countries where they have more confidence. During this period, jobs would be lost. Families would suffer. The National institute of Economic and Social Research (Niesr) is an independent think tank. In a report published on Thursday, it painted a worst case scenario in which the poor would suffer most if we left the EU – because 'it will be necessary to change tax and spending policies as a result of Brexit.' Low income families could receive up to £5542 per year less in tax credits and benefit payments in 2020. This is not a price worth paying. One of Wales' most successful entrepreneurs, Sir Terry Matthews, has branded Brexit an 'absolute disaster'.

The benefits of EU funding for Wales and of freedom of movement for future employment opportunities are unequivocally asserted, supported with simple factual data and clear reasoning. The rhetorical force of the article lies in its direct address from editors to audience: its enticing '9 reasons why' affirmative list style – so familiar to the popular style of online news formats – and its denial of Leave campaign claims any space or agenda-setting power within the article. It may the case that a pro-remain editorial statement was always planned, but perhaps it is also indicative of the difficulties in managing Leave's influence upon and success in framing the discussions within news agendas that such an intervention should have been deemed necessary at Media Wales.

Whilst the factual weight of the argument may appear to have been clearly with Remain within the news discourse (overall, leaving the EU was far more commonly connected with poverty in the economics- and politics-themed coverage (n=162) than remaining (n=31)), this does not mean that, emotionally, the force and direction of the discussion was so clear cut. Whilst emotive language was a feature of news surrounding both sides in the debate, Leave moves to align with the most vulnerable, disenfranchised social groups appealed much more explicitly to antagonistic feelings, including pain, frustration and outrage associated with the perceived injustices of the status quo. These feelings were arraigned against the 'elites' and experts associated with Remain. The emotional tenor of the debate was especially heightened in the week leading up to the vote, with personal testimony pieces, letters and opinion pieces featuring a range of final pleas to voters. Anxiety and alarm concerning livelihoods figure large in this coverage, alongside anger at campaign opponents and fears connected with either outcome of the vote. In a 16 June letter to the *Daily Post*, for example, Dave Haskell from Cardigan exclaims, 'What a despicable, duplicitous and bullying Prime Minister David Cameron is turning out to be – now he is trying to terrify the elderly about their pensions if they do not vote to stay in the EU – what next, an attack on the disabled?' By contrast, a 15 June Wales Online piece that seeks, perhaps rather desperately, to invoke and link nationalistic sentiment with allegiance to the EU, draws an analogy between 'remaining' and the successful run of the Welsh men's football team in the 2016 UEFA football tournament:

> Gareth Bale and the gang will be doing all they can to avoid 'WEXIT' tomorrow, and we'll all be behind them. Politics – of course – is a little more complicated. But voting to leave the EU next Thursday would be even more crushing to Welsh identity and pride than being kicked out of the Euros. (Former BBC chief political correspondent and communications director for Boris Johnson, Guto Harri)

The final week of the campaign also saw the appearance of UKIP's now infamous 'Breaking Point' poster, picturing a long line of refugees accompanied by the text 'The EU has failed us all. We must break free of the EU and take back control of our borders'. A Wales Online piece, 'Farage Under Fire but Unrepentant for Migrants Poster' (16 June), features both Farage's claim that the EU's response to the migrant crisis 'made a fundamental error that risks the security of everybody' and opposing politicians' 'disgust' (Nicola Sturgeon) and 'fears' (Labour AM Mick Antoniw) about the inflammatory impact of such anti-immigration rhetoric, 'feeding a "growing ugly underbelly" of racism in Wales'. Anxieties also featured in the news discourse in less antagonistic modes, deployed in efforts to persuade rather than consolidate existing positions. For example, in 'Why I'm Voting Remain on June 23, by the Social Entrepreneur

Who Brought 150 Jobs to the Valleys' (Wales Online, 16 June), Patrick Nash makes the case for continuing EU membership, adopting an empathetic tone towards Leave sympathisers:

> I posted my vote for the EU Referendum last weekend. I voted to Remain, yet I'm feeling anxious that this isn't enough … I wonder how many people realise they have the EU to thank for their jobs and livelihoods in this part of the world? … My nearest town had the heart ripped out of it many years ago and has struggled to recover economically. Does that mean that many people feel alienated? Of course it does and rightly so. Messages about a growing economy mean nothing when your town or community struggles.

When we look more closely at how news pieces published in the aftermath of the vote were framed, a range of reflections are included seeking to understand the outcome and its potential impact on livelihoods. In 'Here's How People in the Valleys Feel after Voting to Leave the EU' (Wales Online, 28 June), for example, serious uncertainties and concern surrounding the prudence of voting decisions feature prominently, positioned as justified anxieties. Quotes from 'Leave voters', for example: 'We don't know what will happen in the future and I'm now worried about things going wrong', appear alongside those of 'Remainers': 'Now that we are out a lot of people are panicking. I didn't expect people to vote Leave. We have had a lot of help here. Westminster won't give us money and I trust Brussels more than Westminster to give back to Wales'.

In other articles, anger and upset at the result is plainly expressed, even if featured alongside resolution that it should be upheld. In 'We Must Honour the Brexit Vote: Now Let's See the Small Print', for example, Dafydd Wigley contends:

> Britain is poorer today than it was last Thursday. The pound slumped, billions were wiped off pension funds and Britain's credit ratings were slashed. Financial institutions are moving jobs abroad; industrial projects suspended. This was totally foreseeable – and was foreseen. Such warnings – given by 'experts' – were rejected. Some people preferred the economic assessment of Joe Bloggs in the local pub over that of international economic analysts. The chickens have come home to roost. Ordinary working persons – particularly the young seeking jobs and homes – will pay the price. (*Daily Post*, 30 June)

In 'Is Fascism Back to Stalk Our Streets' (*Western Mail*, 1 July), for example, letter writer Gillian Barrar writes of her shame at the result:

> We have betrayed our young people, who are facing a tough, competitive world. They are burdened with debt without the benefits my generation have enjoyed. We, who have had free education and healthcare and pretty decent benefits. Our parents worked and sacrificed to ensure

these benefits for us. Our university was famously funded by 'the pennies of the poor'. Aneurin Bevan built on the tireless work of voluntary committees and dedicated efforts of Miners' Welfare groups to deliver the NHS ... Now the children of that generation, who should know better, through selfishness and narrow self interest have fallen for the dangerous claptrap of Farage and his ilk.

Far less evident in the coverage following the vote were jubilant or confident voices assuring news audiences that the decision to leave the EU would bring economic benefit to Wales or positively impact on ordinary people's livelihoods.

Issues and experiences of poverty

Across our sample, we looked both at the specific issues mentioned relating to poverty, as well as the issues directly reported as experienced by people featured in the article. By examining poverty from these two slightly differing perspectives we aimed to focus upon the degree to which particular issues may be personalised or reported more abstractly in the coverage.

Table 7: Poverty-related issues included in the coverage (as % of news items).

	TV	Radio	Print	Online	All media
Unemployment/jobs	51.9% (n=140)	40.9% (n=117)	44.7% (n=185)	50.4% (n=266)	47.3% (n=708)
Social/welfare funding cuts	23.3% (n=63)	23.4% (n=67)	22.5% (n=93)	26.7% (n=141)	24.3% (n=364)
Poor economy/ infrastructure	27% (n=73)	25.9% (n=74)	12.3% (n=51)	20.8% (n=110)	20.6% (n=308)
Poverty and deprivation	7.4% (n=20)	17.1% (n=49)	24.2% (n=100)	13.3% (n=70)	16% (n=239)
Cost of living (general)	11.5% (n=31)	22% (n=63)	10.1% (n=42)	12.1% (n=64)	13.4% (n=200)
Low wages	10% (n=27)	14.3% (n=41)	14.5% (n=60)	11% (n=58)	12.4% (n=186)
Education problems	13.3% (n=36)	14.7% (n=42)	5.8% (n=24)	15.9% (n=84)	12.4% (n=186)
Pensions	7.8% (n=21)	7.3% (n=21)	20% (n=83)	8.9% (n=47)	11.5% (n=172)
Inequality	10% (n=27)	8.4% (n=24)	19.3% (n=80)	7% (n=37)	11.2% (n=168)

contd.

Table 7: *contd.*

	TV	Radio	Print	Online	All media
Access to benefits	8.5% (n=23)	12.9% (n=37)	10.6% (n=44)	8.7% (n=46)	10% (n=150)
Child poverty	5.9% (n=16)	10.5% (n=30)	9.2% (n=38)	12.1% (n=64)	9.9% (n=148)
Health problems	9.3% (n=25)	13.6% (n=39)	8.5% (n=35)	9.3% (n=49)	9.9% (n=148)
Housing problems	5.9% (n=16)	6.6% (n=19)	11.8% (n=49)	11.6% (n=61)	9.7% (n=145)
Homelessness	5.2% (n=14)	4.5% (n=13)	12.6% (n=52)	6.8% (n=36)	7.7% (n=115)
Rural poverty	11.5% (n=31)	17.1% (n=49)	2.9% (n=12)	4.2% (n=22)	7.6% (n=114)
Other	2.6% (n=7)	5.2% (n=15)	5.6% (n=23)	12.7% (n=67)	7.5% (n=112)
Underemployment	7% (n=19)	10.5% (n=30)	6.5% (n=27)	5.9% (n=31)	7.1% (n=107)
Debt	4.4% (n=12)	7.7% (n=22)	7% (n=29)	6.1% (n=32)	6.3% (n=95)
Cost of transport	7% (n=19)	7% (n=20)	3.6% (n=15)	7% (n=37)	6.1% (n=91)
Hunger	4.4% (n=8)	8.7% (n=25)	4.3% (n=18)	4.7% (n=25)	5.1% (n=76)
Household bills	7% (n=6)	25.2% (n=15)	5.3% (n=22)	5.1% (n=27)	4.7% (n=70)
Benefit levels	4.4% (n=13)	2.1% (n=6)	7% (n=29)	3.4% (n=18)	4.4% (n=66)
Access to credit	7% (n=10)	5.6% (n=16)	0.2% (n=1)	1.9% (n=10)	2.5% (n=37)
Cost of childcare	1.9% (n=5)	3.8% (n=11)	2.7% (n=11)	1.9% (n=10)	2.5% (n=37)
Rent levels	1.9% (n=5)	2.4% (n=7)	1.2% (n=5)	2.7% (n=14)	2.1% (n=31)
Food banks	0.7% (n=2)	2.8% (n=8)	3.4% (n=14)	0.8% (n=4)	1.9% (n=28)
Forced labour/ slavery	1.1% (n=3)	0% (n=0)	1.2% (n=5)	0.8% (n=4)	0.8% (n=12)
No specific issue mentioned	0.7% (n=2)	0% (n=0)	0.2% (n=1)	0.2% (n=1)	0.3% (n=4)
Total	(n=674)	(n=860)	(n=1148)	(n=1435)	(n=4117)

When we examine the coverage, we see a diversity of issues associated with poverty. Overall, 4,117 issues were recorded across the 1,498 news items in our sample. By far the most commonly cited issue was that of unemployment/jobs – present in 47.3% of all news items (n=708), followed by social/welfare funding cuts (24.3%, n=364) and a poor economy/infrastructure (20.6%, n=308).

When we look at the issues reported as experiences of people, the picture is slightly different, with a narrower range of particular issues represented and the most significant category across media types identified as 'experiencing poverty/social exclusion' in general terms (n=460, 30.7% of news items). However, in other respects the experiences reported mirror the poverty-related issues detailed in Table 7 above, with employment insecurity (28.9%, n=433) and unemployment (28.3%, n=424) featuring strongly across media, alongside problems or difficulties in accessing benefits and services (22.9% of news items, n=343), which included problems associated with changes to benefits and social/welfare funding cuts more generally.

Table 8: Poverty experiences across media (as % of news items).

	Television	Radio	Print	Online	All media
Poverty/social exclusion (in general)	15.2% (n=41)	32.2% (n=92)	30.9% (n=128)	37.7% (n=199)	30.7% (n=460)
Employment insecurity	34.8% (n=94)	28% (n=80)	22.7% (n=94)	31.3% (n=165)	28.9% (n=433)
Unemployment	27.8% (n=75)	21% (n=60)	26.3% (n=109)	34.1% (n=180)	28.3% (n=424)
Accessing benefits and services	26.3% (n=71)	31.1% (n=89)	22.9% (n=95)	16.7% (n=88)	22.9% (n=343)
Health (mental/physical)	10.7% (n=29)	8.7% (n=25)	14% (n=58)	16.1% (n=85)	13.2% (n=197)
No experiences featured	15.9% (n=43)	8% (n=23)	14.3% (n=59)	8.7% (n=46)	11.4% (n=171)
Other	4.8% (n=13)	7.7% (n=22)	8.9% (n=37)	15% (n=79)	10.1% (n=151)
Low wages	7% (n=19)	7.7% (n=22)	12.1% (n=50)	9.7% (n=51)	9.5% (n=142)
Pension insecurity	5.9% (n=16)	4.2% (n=12)	13% (n=54)	6.1% (n=32)	7.6% (n=114)
Homelessness	2.6% (n=7)	5.2% (n=15)	11.8% (n=49)	5.5% (n=29)	6.7% (n=100)
Underemployment	5.2% (n=14)	3.5% (n=10)	2.7% (n=11)	2.3% (n=12)	3.1% (n=47)
Total	156.3% (n=422)	157.3% (n=450)	179.7% (n=744)	183% (n=966)	172.4%[1] (n=2582)

Whilst the frequencies in different types of experiences of poverty were reasonably consistent across media types, some categories of experience did feature more strongly in some sections of the media than others. For example, whilst homelessness was not very frequently profiled as an experience overall, it was covered far more often in print (11.8% of news items, n=49) than in broadcast media (television: 2.6% of news items, n=7); radio: 5.2% of news items, n=15) or online (29% of news items, n=29). In 11.4% of news items overall (n=171), no explicit references to experiences of poverty were made at all, suggesting a more abstract or depersonalised form of coverage of the issues. This was more likely to be the case on television (15.9%, n=43) and in print news (14.3%, n=59) than radio (8%, n=23) or online news coverage (8.7%, n=46).

Causes and consequences of poverty

To further explore the framework within which poverty and associated issues were reported, we analysed what, if any, causes or reasons were attached to poverty and its related issues in the coverage. In 27.3% of news items (n=409), no causes at all were mentioned.

Table 9: Causes of poverty-related issues by media type (as % of news items).

	Television	Radio	Print	Online	All media
No causes featured	28.9% (n=78)	21% (n=60)	28.3% (n=117)	29.2% (n=154)	27.3% (n=409)
Structural	18.1% (n=49)	21% (n=60)	19.8% (n=82)	19.1% (n=101)	19.5% (n=292)
Wales economy/ deindustrialisation	16.3% (n=44)	19.9% (n=57)	11.8% (n=49)	18.9% (n=100)	16.7% (n=250)
Voting to leave EU/ Brexit	14.1% (n=38)	12.2% (n=35)	15% (n=62)	15.7% (n=83)	14.6% (n=218)
Funding cuts/ austerity measures[2]	15.2% (n=41)	13.6% (n=39)	8.9% (n=37)	12.5% (n=66)	12.2% (n=183)
Business practices/ actions of corporations	10.7% (n=29)	11.5% (n=33)	14.3% (n=59)	7.6% (n=40)	10.7% (n=161)
Globalisation	9.3% (n=25)	8.7% (n=25)	8.2% (n=34)	9.7% (n=51)	9% (n=135)
Individual	4.1% (n=11)	5.2% (n=15)	7.7% (n=32)	7.8% (n=41)	6.6% (n=99)

contd.

Table 9: *contd.*

	Television	Radio	Print	Online	All media
China/India	3% (n=8)	3.8% (n=11)	5.8% (n=24)	5.7% (n=30)	4.9% (n=73)
Fuel/energy costs	5.2% (n=14)	3.5% (n=10)	5.1% (n=21)	4.4% (n=23)	4.5% (n=68)
Other	3.3% (n=9)	3.5% (n=10)	4.8% (n=20)	4.7% (n=25)	4.3% (n=64)
Voting to remain in EU/EU membership	4.8% (n=13)	2.4% (n=7)	4.8% (n=20)	4.2% (n=22)	4.1% (n=62)
Transportation	3.3% (n=9)	4.9% (n=14)	1.4% (n=6)	1.9% (n=10)	2.6% (n=39)
Substance dependence	0.4% (n=1)	0% (n=0)	4.6% (n=19)	2.1% (n=11)	2.1% (n=31)
War or conflict	0.7% (n=2)	3.1% (n=9)	2.4% (n=10)	0% (n=0)	1.4% (n=21)
Worklessness[3]	0.4% (n=1)	0% (n=0)	0.5% (n=2)	0.4% (n=2)	0.3% (n=5)
Total	137.8% (n=372)	134.6% (n=385)	143.5% (n=594)	143.8% (n=759)	140.9% (n=2110)

However, in the 72.7% (n=1089) of news items that did imply or explicitly feature causes, overwhelmingly it was structural[4] or macroeconomic causes that were identified as causing poverty.

We can say that there was significantly more emphasis in the coverage upon structural causes (27.3% of news items, n=292) and problems associated with the Welsh economy/deindustrialisation as causal factors for poverty (16.7% of news items, n=250) than upon the behaviour of individuals represented as a cause of their own poverty (6.6% of news items, n=99) or certain cultural norms of 'worklessness', implying an insufficient work ethic amongst the poor (0.3% of news items, n=5). Indeed, we saw little, if any, evidence of people experiencing poverty being framed in an overtly stereotyping or stigmatising during our monitoring period.

Whilst our sample does not represent all of the news coverage of Brexit in Wales during the periods monitored, it does capture all coverage relating to poverty, economic inequality and discussion of the potential impacts of the outcome of the referendum on livelihoods and social deprivation in Wales. Like the coverage more generally, it may be that, whilst issues relevant to possible or probable causes of poverty may commonly have been implicit within news narratives, they were not always explicitly framed as such (although, as explored above, there were notable exceptions). In other words, the data suggests

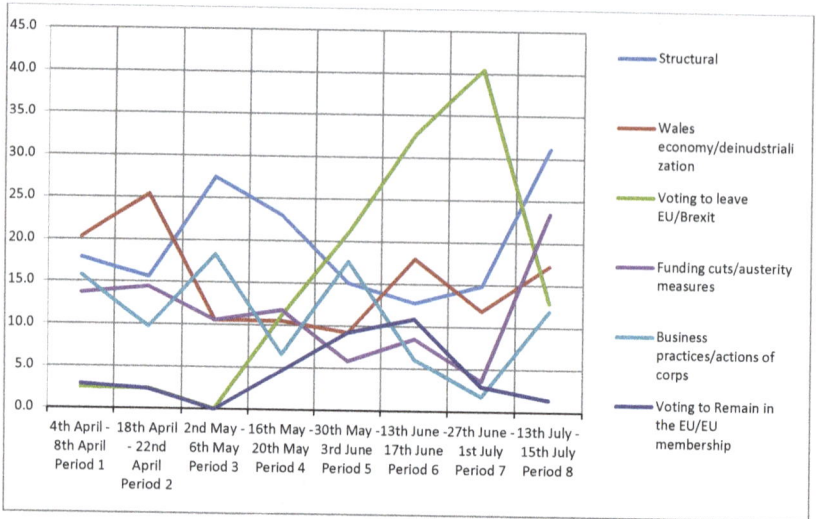

Figure 4: Causes of poverty from April to July 2016 (as % of all media coverage).

that complex and disputed structural or economic questions (such as the consequences of Brexiting or not Brexiting) often were not explicitly connected to what they might mean, concretely, in the everyday realities of people's lives.

When references to EU membership and referendum voting decisions were identified, both 'voting to leave the EU/Brexit' (14.6% of news items, n=218) and EU membership in the past or present and/or 'voting to remain in the EU/EU membership' (4.1% of news items, n=62) were positioned as either a cause of current insecurities, potential future deprivation/poorer livelihoods or a curb on prosperity – polarised positions largely introduced to the coverage by sources on opposing sides of the referendum campaign. However, whilst frequencies in the representation of 'leaving' and 'remaining' as causes of poverty both escalated during the weeks of the referendum campaign in May and June, 'Voting to leave the EU/Brexit' escalated much more sharply, continuing in the immediate aftermath of the vote to reach a peak in Coding Period 7 (40.5% of news items, n=68), before abating in July.

The framing of 'voting to remain/EU membership' as a potential cause of poverty, by comparison, reached a much lesser, but nonetheless significant peak in Coding Period 6 – prior to the referendum vote (10.9% of news items, n=23). It may not be surprising that coverage of concerns relating to poverty linked with Brexit in the news in Wales far outweighed coverage of concerns linked with remaining, given that Wales has been a net beneficiary of EU funding in recent years. On the other hand, given the outcome of the vote in Wales, it may appear that this aspect of the coverage was out of step with public opinion. However, most notably, it is clear that very little poverty coverage featuring causal framing relating to the issue of EU membership appeared at all until

Table 10: Consequences of poverty across media[5] (as % of news items).

	Television	Radio	Print	Online	All media
No consequences featured	48.9% (n=132)	29% (n=83)	38.4% (n=159)	24.6% (n=130)	33.6% (n=504)
Communities suffer	27.4% (n=74)	33.6% (n=96)	23.7% (n=98)	41.1% (n=217)	32.4% (n=485)
Low household incomes	10.4% (n=28)	20.6% (n=59)	19.6% (n=81)	18.9% (n=100)	17.9% (n=268)
Social exclusion[6]	12.6% (n=34)	21.3% (n=61)	14.7% (n=61)	18.2% (n=96)	16.8% (n=252)
Social/economic Inequality	5.9% (n=16)	16.4% (n=47)	13.5% (n=56)	20.8% (n=110)	15.3% (n=229)
Health problems	9.6% (n=26)	9.8% (n=28)	18.6% (n=77)	16.3% (n=86)	14.5% (n=217)
Children/families suffer	9.3% (n=25)	10.5% (n=30)	11.6% (n=48)	15.9% (n=84)	12.5% (n=187)
Educational problems	6.7% (n=18)	3.5% (n=10)	4.3% (n=18)	8.7% (n=46)	6.1% (n=92)
Other	1.1% (n=3)	1.4% (n=4)	4.6% (n=19)	4.5% (n=24)	3.3% (n=50)
Total	131.9% (n=356)	146.2% (n=418)	149% (n=617)	169.1% (n=893)	152.5% (n=2284)

Coding Period 4 – the latter half of May and deep into the campaign itself. This indicates that a strong narrative framework of understanding about poverty and the potential impacts upon livelihoods of Brexiting or not Brexiting may not have developed in the months leading up to the vote. Rather, the news narrative on EU membership versus Brexit in relation to poverty was framed more through intensive coverage of the issues during a relatively brief period of weeks immediately preceding it.

In order to further consider how coverage was framed, we also examined what, if any, consequences were identified as resulting from poverty. In other words, how, if at all, did the effects of poverty on individuals, their communities or wider society feature in news stories?

Overall, 33.6% of news items (n=504) did not directly mention or draw attention to any consequences of poverty, which means that the implications of poverty or the experiences resulting from it for individuals, their communities or wider society did not feature either explicitly or implicitly in the narrative.

In the 66.4% of news items (n=995) that did include references to the consequences of poverty, both general societal and more localised or individuated issues were identified. The most frequently mentioned consequence was the broad idea that communities suffer (32.4%, n=485). This included coverage where job losses in an area were framed in terms of how the local community or region might be impacted, for example the detrimental effects upon the whole area of a bus company in Flintshire going into administration, or when actual or threatened job losses, industrial uncertainties or crises were feared to impact the prospects of a whole community (e.g. in some 'Circuit of Wales' and Tata Steel crisis stories). Low household incomes also featured significantly across the coverage (17.9% of causes identified, n=268), as did social/economic inequality (15.3%, n=229). It is worth noting that some of the 16.8% (n=252) of coverage relating to either 'social exclusion' or ideas about 'opportunities' and 'life chances' were brought into the coverage by political figures (for example, in stories about Conservative Stephen Crabb's leadership campaign positions connecting his personal socio-economic background to his policy positions; Jeremy Corbyn's explanations of his policy positions on socio-economic disadvantage in defending his leadership; and points made about Theresa May's reflections on the consequences of poverty in her first speech as PM). Aside from such high-profile examples, very few stories profiling the consequences of poverty for specific individuals, for example through interviews or more extensive case studies, featured in the coverage.

Responsibility for poverty

We also examined how, if at all, responsibility for poverty was represented, either directly or clearly implied in the coverage. In 26.4% of news items (n=396) no responsibility was suggested or attributed at all for poverty. This was highest in print (31.2% of articles, n=129), followed by online (25.9%, n=137) and television (24.4%, n=66), and lowest in radio coverage (22.4%, n=64). However, in the 73.6% (n=1102) of the coverage across all media where responsibility did feature, it was the Welsh Assembly Government that was most frequently positioned as bearing or taking responsibility (19.8% of news items, n=296), followed by private interests/business (17.6%, n=264) and then the then UK national government (16.2%, n=242). This is interesting, as, although many of the areas that might be associated with preventing or alleviating poverty, such as economic development, social welfare and housing, are devolved areas of policy to the Welsh Assembly Government, other key policy areas conditioning or affecting poverty such as employment and social security and the UK tax system remain in the power of the government at Westminster. Far fewer stories placed responsibility for poverty with local government, with some of those that did focusing on tackling or managing homelessness.

Individuals were far less likely than government and other institutions to be positioned as responsible for the poverty issues affecting them (5.9% of poverty attributions, n=88), although this was slightly more frequent in print (8.7%, n=36) than other media types. In this we can see little evidence that the kinds of stigmatising narratives about those experiencing poverty that previous research has identified as a characteristic of coverage in key sections of the UK national press.

Interestingly, the public's voting behaviour in the EU referendum also featured significantly in the way that responsibility for poverty was identified across the coverage, with people voting for Brexit more strongly positioned as responsible (13.8%, n=207) than those voting to remain in the EU (2.5%, n=37). These findings can be generally understood to capture something of the moral tone of stories on poverty. Although identified at a lower frequency overall, they broadly mirror the data presented above on the objective 'causes of poverty' identified in the coverage (where 14.6% (n=218) of coverage featured leaving the EU as a potential cause of poverty, whilst only 4.1% (n=62) of coverage identified remaining).

Table 11: Responsibility attributions for poverty (as % of news items).

	Television	Radio	Print	Online	All media
No responsibility featured	24.4% (n=66)	22.4% (n=64)	31.2% (n=129)	25.9% (n=137)	26.4% (n=396)
WAG policy	29.3% (n=79)	24.8% (n=71)	13.8% (n=57)	16.9% (n=89)	19.8% (n=296)
Private interests/ business	18.5% (n=50)	18.2% (n=52)	16.4% (n=68)	17.8% (n=94)	17.6% (n=264)
National government policy (present)	9.6% (n=26)	13.3% (n=38)	19.8% (n=82)	18.2% (n=96)	16.2% (n=242)
Voting to leave EU	10% (n=27)	9.4% (n=27)	14.3% (n=59)	17.8% (n=94)	13.8% (n=207)
EU policy	9.6% (n=26)	9.1% (n=26)	8% (n=33)	6.6% (n=35)	8% (n=120)
Local government policy	9.3% (n=25)	9.4% (n=27)	4.8% (n=20)	7.6% (n=40)	7.5% (n=112)
National government policy (past)	4.1% (n=11)	5.2% (n=15)	8.7% (n=36)	7.6% (n=40)	6.8% (n=102)
Individuals affected	3.3% (n=9)	2.8% (n=8)	8.7% (n=36)	6.6% (n=35)	5.9% (n=88)
Other	4.8% (n=13)	5.9% (n=17)	4.8% (n=20)	4.7% (n=25)	5% (n=75)
Voting to remain in EU	0.7% (n=2)	0.3% (n=1)	3.6% (n=15)	3.6% (n=19)	2.5% (n=37)
Total	123.7% (n=334)	121% (n=346)	134.1% (n=555)	133.3% (n=704)	129.4% (n=1939)

Responses to poverty

In addition to the 'responsibility' attributed for poverty and poverty-related issues, we also examined the coverage for the 'responses to poverty' that were included in the coverage as actions that were being, could or should be taken. Responses of some kind were suggested in the majority of the news items in our sample (90.4%, n=1354). These were fairly wide-ranging but focused largely on governmental intervention at the Welsh Assembly (26.5%, n=397) or UK government (21.5%, n=322) levels, as well as in political campaigns for change that were targeted at those levels of government (18.4%, n=275) and which largely related to campaigning in the run-up to the Welsh Government elections. There was also significant emphasis upon the responses that could be or were being made by business (20.9%, n=313). We found little emphasis upon responses taken or expected of individuals ('pull yourself up by the bootstraps' kind of narratives), with 'individual action' making up only 3.9% (n=59) of coded responses. Similarly, law and order responses were not often proposed (5.9%, n=88) and, rather than relate to the policing of those in poverty, those that did feature related mainly to action to tackle scams, prevent defrauding people of their savings or challenge modern slavery. Specific calls for changes to benefits and/or the minimum wage were coded separately, and, although both raising (2.5%, n=38) and cutting welfare benefit levels (0.9%, n=14) were proposed in news articles as responses to poverty (reflecting the inclusion of differing political/ideological stances on policy responses included in reporting), these featured infrequently in the coverage in comparison to more general calls for government interventions.

Table 12: Responses to poverty (as % of news items).

	TV	Radio	Print	Online	All media
Welsh Assembly Government intervention	30.7% (n=83)	29.7% (n=85)	23.4% (n=97)	25% (n=132)	26.5% (n=397)
UK government intervention	23% (n=62)	18.5% (n=53)	27.3% (n=113)	17.8% (n=94)	21.5% (n=322)
Private/business intervention	21.9% (n=59)	14.3% (n=41)	19.6% (n=81)	25% (n=132)	20.9% (n=313)
Political campaign	21.9% (n=59)	20.6% (n=59)	13.5% (n=60)	18.4% (n=97)	18.4% (n=275)
Charitable project	3.3% (n=9)	4.9% (n=14)	13.8% (n=57)	12.3% (n=65)	9.7% (n=145)
No response featured	10.7% (n=29)	13.6% (n=39)	7.5% (n=31)	8.5% (n=45)	9.6% (n=144)
EU remain vote	9.3% (n=25)	11.5% (n=33)	8.9% (n=37)	9.1% (n=48)	9.5% (n=143)

contd.

Table 12: *contd.*

	TV	Radio	Print	Online	All media
Local government intervention	8.1% (n=22)	7% (n=20)	7.7% (n=32)	10.6% (n=56)	8.7% (n=130)
Other	4.8% (n=13)	8% (n=23)	6.3% (n=26)	10.8% (n=57)	7.9% (n=119)
Law and order	5.6% (n=15)	1.7% (n=5)	9.9% (n=41)	5.1% (n=27)	5.9% (n=88)
EU leave vote	6.3% (n=17)	4.9% (n=14)	5.3% (n=22)	5.3% (n=28)	5.4% (n=81)
Protest	7.4% (n=20)	3.1% (n=9)	3.4% (n=14)	6.6% (n=35)	5.2% (n=78)
Union action	6.7% (n=18)	2.4% (n=7)	6.3% (n=26)	4.7% (n=25)	5.1% (n=76)
Individual action	2.2% (n=6)	0.7% (n=2)	4.6% (n=19)	6.1% (n=32)	3.9% (n=59)
Charitable contribution	0.4% (n=1)	1.4% (n=4)	3.4% (n=14)	5.1% (n=27)	3.1% (n=46)
Raise benefits levels	3% (n=8)	3.1% (n=9)	3.6% (n=15)	1.1% (n=6)	2.5% (n=38)
Art and culture	1.1% (n=3)	0.3% (n=1)	1% (n=4)	1.5% (n=8)	1.1% (n=16)
Cut benefit levels	1.5% (n=4)	0.7% (n=2)	1.4% (n=6)	0.4% (n=2)	0.9% (n=14)
Raise minimum/ living wage	0% (n=0)	0% (n=0)	1% (n=4)	0.6% (n=3)	0.5% (n=7)
Other	0.7% (n=2)	0% (n=0)	0% (n=0)	0.2% (n=1)	0.2% (n=3)
Total	168.5% (n=455)	146.9% (n=420)	168.8% (n=699)	174.2% (n=920)	166.5% (n=2494)

In this category, we again saw the issue of Brexit figure reasonably significantly, with findings again corroborating the data presented above. Here, voting to remain as a response to possible impoverishment or threatened livelihoods featured in 9.5% of news items across media types (n=143), whilst voting to leave featured less frequently (5.4% of coverage, n=81).

When we look more closely at coverage identifying the Welsh Government as bearing responsibility for the poverty issues featured, we see that these issues are not always confined to policy areas currently devolved to the Welsh Government. Whilst Welsh Government powers may allow it to mitigate any potential impacts of UK government welfare policies in Wales in various ways (for example through targeted policies in education or health), in 2016 at least, the Welsh

Government did not have significant tax raising powers, or to introduce large-scale welfare reforms or to control the administration of important welfare payments.[7] However, a sense of Welsh Government responsibility for poverty issues beyond the remit of powers in Wales can sometimes be conveyed in reporting, in various ways. In some articles, issues framed as the responsibility of UK national government were often responded to by Welsh Government spokespeople, seeking to highlight strategic interventions in Wales. For example, in 'Call to Give the Seaside a Tsar to Fight Decay' (*Daily Post*, 11 July) the British Hospitality Association's (BHA) call for national interventions, including a VAT cut for tourism, is profiled. Alongside a call from a Llandudno hotelier for more to be done 'for politicians in Cardiff and Westminster', a Welsh Government spokesman is cited:

> We are lucky in Wales to have a truly magnificent coastline with unparalleled views and attractions and we are determined to help our coastal communities to make the most of their areas' natural features, enhance their potential and drive local growth and jobs. Our Vibrant and Viable Places capital fund is helping many coastal towns and just earlier this week we invited applications for the £3.4m Big Lottery fund's Coastal Communities Fund.

With no similar response included in the article from a national government spokesperson, arguably the focus of responsibility for BHA concerns, 'to help towns "fight back from decades of decay"', is disproportionately steered towards the Welsh Government. Similarly, in 'Nurses Tell of Fears over Patient Health' (*Western Mail*, 28 June), a UK-wide Royal College of Nursing (RCN) survey of nurses' and health care assistants' views on health care challenges is reported, with a particular focus on its significance for Wales. Tina Donnelly, director of RCN Wales, is quoted, offering her analysis of the survey's findings:

> Those surveyed are telling us that the health of their patients is deteriorating due to social inequalities such as poor housing or poverty – intolerable issues that we would expect to be tackled more effectively in modern-day Britain ... We must strengthen the public health agenda by increasing funding in Wales for key areas such as housing and social benefits to those who are truly in need. Ultimately we must ensure that the inequalities which currently divide those with good and poor health become a thing of the past so that every member of the public is given the same opportunities in regard to their ongoing health and wellbeing.

With attention firmly on the desired outcomes and a collective need ('we must...') to address social inequalities, and in the absence of any further framing journalistic commentary, the attribution of responsibility for making these goals a reality in Wales becomes rather generalised.

Indeed, the dividing lines between Welsh and UK national government powers (and therefore a sense of who should be held to account) are not always apparent in articles. The boundary can often be blurred, largely as a result of rhetorical choices by politicians quoted in the news item seeking to attach significance to their claims – an unsurprising feature of reporting during campaigning in the run-up to the election and EU referendum vote, for example, but also evident in other areas of the coverage. In the midst of the crisis facing Port Talbot steelworkers, First Minister Carwyn Jones emphasised his active role in negotiations and a possible deal for Port Talbot, in 'Steel Crisis Offer Welcomed by Industry and Unions':

> We're committed to supporting any credible bid to secure steel making in Wales. We have worked with the UK Government to put in place this significant package of support and we believe that this will help secure a successful sale of Tata Steel's operations in Wales and the rest of the UK. (*Daily Post*, 22 April)

Here, the collective 'we' again obscures the dynamics of power and potential responsibility for the prospects of the plant and the livelihoods of workers and their families dependent upon it.

The question of the degree to which the Welsh Government can effectively address poverty and affect livelihoods through the 'levers' at its disposal remains a live policy issue. It is also one of significant complexity that is difficult to measure and to separate from the far-reaching impact in Wales of policies instituted by the UK national government at Westminster. In journalistic discourse, where the focus of a story is rarely *primarily* one of measuring degrees of responsibility applicable to different levels of government in the devolved system, it is perhaps unsurprising, then, that the framing of responsibility for poverty-related issues might be lacking in clarity. Yet, this does not mean that it is unimportant: if journalism is to address its fourth estate role on poverty effectively in Wales, it may be essential to develop ways in which its complexity can be more meaningfully and holistically understood in the public discourse, including frameworks for discerning political accountability.

Voices on poverty

Finally, we examined the types of people who were quoted directly indirectly as sources in each news item. Sources were cited in the majority of news items in our sample (93.1%, n=1394). All sources cited within each news item were counted (n=4323), with multiple sources appearing within most (63.2%, n=946). The largest category of sources was political figures or parties (35.6% of sources, n=1540) followed by ordinary citizens/residents (18.9%, n=819) and then business sources (13.6%, n=587). Media sources also appear to be fairly significant in our sample, but this is largely due to the coding of broadcast news where links between anchors and journalists were also coded as sources. Although broadly these trends were consistent across media types, notably political sources were most prevalent in print news (44.9% of print sources, n=508), whilst ordinary citizens/residents were cited significantly more frequently in television news (29.6% of television sources, n=299) than in other media. Similarly, but on a lesser scale, business voices were most likely to be heard in online news (18.3% of online sources, n=273), whilst the third sector was more likely to be cited in print (8% of print sources, n=90) than in other media.

Table 13: Sources included in the coverage (% of total sources).

	Television	Radio	Print	Online	All media
Political source	28.2% (n=285)	32% (n=221)	44.9% (n=508)	35.3% (n=526)	35.6% (n=1540)
Ordinary citizens/ residents	29.6% (n=299)	18.7% (n=129)	11.1% (n=125)	17.8% (n=266)	18.9% (n=819)
Business	9.8% (n=99)	9.6% (n=66)	13.2% (n=149)	18.3% (n=273)	13.6% (n=587)
Media	14.8% (n=149)	13.7% (n=95)	1.9% (n=22)	3.6% (n=53)	7.4% (n=319)
Third sector	2.7% (n=27)	4.6% (n=32)	8% (n=90)	3.8% (n=56)	4.7% (n=205)
Union	4.1% (n=41)	4.5% (n=31)	4.8% (n=54)	4.3% (n=64)	4.4% (n=190)
Law and order	0.9% (n=9)	0.3% (n=2)	5.7% (n=65)	3.6% (n=54)	3% (n=130)
Report	1.7% (n=17)	2.7% (n=19)	3.3% (n=37)	3.5% (n=52)	2.9% (n=125)
Academic	2.4% (n=24)	4.6% (n=32)	1.4% (n=16)	3% (n=45)	2.7% (n=117)
Education	3.1% (n=31)	3% (n=21)	1% (n=11)	3% (n=45)	2.5% (n=108)
Health	1.2% (n=12)	1.4% (n=10)	1.9% (n=21)	1.8% (n=27)	1.6% (n=70)
Other	0.7% (n=7)	1% (n=7)	1.2% (n=14)	1.1% (n=16)	1% (n=44)
Opinion poll	0.1% (n=1)	0.6% (n=4)	0.9% (n=10)	0.6% (n=9)	0.6% (n=24)
Religious figure/ organisation	0.2% (n=2)	0.7% (n=5)	1.4% (n=5)	0.2% (n=3)	0.3% (n=15)
Agriculture	0.6% (n=6)	0.6% (n=4)	0.2% (n=2)	0% (n=0)	0.3% (n=12)
Unidentified source	0.1% (n=1)	1% (n=13)	0.2% (n=2)	0.2% (n=2)	0.3% (n=18)
Total	100% (n=1010)	100% (n=691)	100% (n=1131)	100% (n=1491)	100% (n=4323)

When we look more closely at the political sources included, we see that, overall, UK national politicians are most likely to be cited. However, in this, there was some disparity between print and television news, with print news featuring UK national politicians more frequently than other political sources (18.3% of print sources, n=207), whereas television news featured Welsh Government politicians most frequently (10.9% of television sources, n=110), as did online news (11.7% of online sources, n=174), and radio was most likely to cite 'political parties' more generally (9.3% of radio sources, n=64). Local government sources were less likely to appear as sources across media types, although were most likely to feature online (6.8% of radio sources, n=102) and least likely in television news (3.2% of television sources, n=32).

Ordinary citizens/residents featured prominently as a category of sources identified across news types, but we also examined, in more detail, which citizens/residents were included in that category and whether these were people clearly affected or otherwise by the issues associated with poverty covered in the story. The largest category of citizens/residents represented as sources were those not explicitly identified as having been affected by poverty (6.7% of sources, n=291), with the next biggest category those identified generally as a citizen/resident affected by poverty issues in some way (4.1% of sources, n=176). The next significant category was workers affected by poverty issues (3.5% of sources, n=150), although workers were featured more prominently in television news (6.9% of sources, n=70) than in other media types. Youth were only cited 62 times across the coverage (1.4% of sources) and the inclusion of other more specific demographic groups as sources was even more seldom (at least in terms of how people were identified in the coverage), with the elderly cited 50 times (1.2% of sources), and homeless people and those with a migrant background (including refugees) each cited only six times across the coverage (0.1% of sources).

Table 14: Political sources (% of total sources).

Political sources	Television	Radio	Print	Online	All media
UK national politician	7.1% (n=72)	8.2% (n=57)	18.3% (n=207)	11.3% (n=169)	11.7% (n=505)
Welsh Assembly Government politician	10.9% (n=110)	8.4% (n=58)	13.1% (n=148)	11.7% (n=174)	11.3% (n=490)
Political party	7% (n=71)	9.3% (n=64)	6.9% (n=78)	4.9% (n=73)	6.6% (n=286)
Political source: local government	3.2% (n=32)	3.8% (n=26)	6% (n=68)	6.8% (n=102)	5.3% (n=228)
Political source: international	0% (n=0)	2.3% (n=16)	0.6% (n=7)	0.5% (n=8)	0.7% (n=31)
Total political sources	28.2% (n=285)	32% (n=221)	44.9% (n=508)	35.3% (n=526)	35.6% (n=1540)

Table 15: Ordinary citizens as sources (% of total sources).

Ordinary citizens/ residents	Television	Radio	Print	Online	All media
Ordinary citizen/ resident (other)	9.9% (n=100)	5.1% (n=35)	4.1% (n=46)	7.4% (n=110)	6.7% (n=291)
Ordinary citizen/ resident – affected	5.8% (n=59)	6.4% (n=44)	3.4% (n=39)	2.3% (n=34)	4.1% (n=176)
Worker – affected	6.9% (n=70)	2.6% (n=18)	1.9% (n=22)	2.7% (n=40)	3.5% (n=150)
Youth – affected	2.1% (n=21)	0.9% (n=6)	0.4% (n=4)	2.1% (n=31)	1.4% (n=62)
Parent (other) – affected	1.3% (n=13)	1.7% (n=12)	0.4% (n=4)	1.8% (n=27)	1.3% (n=56)
Elderly – affected	2.8% (n=28)	1.6% (n=11)	0.1% (n=1)	0.7% (n=10)	1.2% (n=50)
Single parent – affected	0.1% (n=1)	0.1% (n=1)	0.4% (n=4)	0.3% (n=5)	0.3% (n=11)
Other unidentified – affected	0.6% (n=6)	0.1% (n=1)	0% (n=0)	0.3% (n=4)	0.3% (n=11)
Homeless person	0% (n=0)	0% (n=0)	0.1% (n=1)	0.3% (n=5)	0.1% (n=6)
Person with migrant back-ground – affected	0.1% (n=1)	0.1% (n=1)	0.4% (n=4)	0% (n=0)	0.1% (n=6)
Total ordinary citizens/residents	29.6% (n=299)	18.7% (n=129)	11.1% (n=125)	17.8% (n=266)	18.9% (n=819)

Gender of sources

To further investigate the dynamics of which voices are heard on poverty issues in the media in Wales, we analysed the gender of sources featured. Strikingly, the findings are fairly consistent across the coverage in that male sources (55.9% of sources, n=2415) far outweigh female (24.7% of sources, n=1069). More than twice the number of male voices to female featured in all media but television news, where male sources comprised 53.8% of sources (n=543) compared with 30.2% of female sources (n=305). In 19.4% of coverage overall, no gender was identified, either because the source was inanimate (e.g. an opinion poll or report), unidentified or identified only by a non-gendered category (e.g. 'workers say'), or where gender was otherwise impossible to reliably identify.

Table 16: Source gender (% of total source gender identified).

	Television	Radio	Print	Online	All media
Male	53.8% (n=543)	52.4% (n=362)	58.6% (n=663)	56.8% (n=847)	55.9% (n=2415)
Female	30.2% (n=305)	26.2% (n=181)	21.3% (n=241)	22.9% (n=342)	24.7% (n=1069)
No gender identified	16.0% (n=162)	21.4% (n=148)	20.1% (n=227)	20.3% (n=302)	19.4% (n=839)
Total	100% (n=1010)	100% (n=691)	100% (n=1131)	100% (n=1491)	100% (n=4323)

Summary of content study

Overall, the media coverage on poverty in Wales is characterised by features that accurately reflect some of the complexities of poverty. However, these features are often embedded within reporting focused on the social, economic and political stories that contextualise poverty at a 'macro' level, such as unemployment or resource budget funding cuts. Indeed, coverage of poverty is thematically focused on news about the economy and/or politics, and during our monitoring, was largely driven by Welsh Government policy/politics, business news and the EU referendum campaign. Only a third of reports featuring poverty focused on it as the main story. In such coverage, there is seldom space to connect the forces at play which impact on the economy and public policy to the impact on people's everyday lives in their communities, or the experiences of families or individual households. Conversely, the coverage that does focus primarily on poverty may powerfully resonate with audiences in terms of experiences 'on the ground' but not necessarily connect with the complex conditioning or 'framing' features that would situate those stories within narratives explaining causes, consequences or responsibility for poverty in Wales. Indeed, the mechanisms for framing stories – through indicating the causes and consequences of poverty, for example, were often (in roughly a third of coverage) not included in reports at all. This is important because such features can embed a level of reasoning and reflection that helps audiences to understand the contexts in which poverty arises and its wider social ramifications. Without such framing, the existence of poverty and the question of responsibility for it is unlikely to be scrutinised, the issue seemingly naturalised as something that just 'is', with little prospect of change.

When specific issues associated with poverty were covered, the main focuses were unemployment and job insecurity, although poverty and social deprivation more generally featured large in the narrative across media. This is perhaps unsurprising, given the big stories during our monitoring including the Tata Steel crisis and a number of business closures. Also notable was the prevailing undercurrent of anxiety that such stories signalled, with varying degrees of directness, due to their focus on precarious employment and uncertainty surrounding Wales's future prospects, especially with the loss of European Union funding after Brexit. Voting to leave the European Union (Brexit) was more likely to be positioned as responsible for poverty or deprivation in the future or as a cause of increasing insecurity than voting to remain/remaining in the EU. However, importantly, the number of stories connecting either Brexit or remaining in the EU to poverty issues was not very significant until well into the referendum campaign. Where coverage did include framing and contextualising features, structural factors, including the legacy for the Welsh economy of deindustrialisation, were positioned as the primary contextualising causes of poverty issues. The most often cited consequence of poverty was the general sense that 'communities suffer' – a feature which, lacking in personal detail, may have been indicative of a distance between those experiencing poverty and journalists in their reporting.

More positively, there was no significant evidence of stigmatising narratives on poverty in the Welsh media, with no notable evidence of vulnerable people or those suffering hardship being blamed for their experiences of poverty, economic inequality or social disadvantage. The categories of people identified as affected by poverty were quite broad, with 'communities' or the public in general more likely to be the reference point than a specific demographic group. Workers who had either lost their jobs or whose jobs were under threat were also a key focus, located in a variety of areas of Wales.

On the question of responsibility for poverty, government, and in particular the Welsh Government, was most frequently positioned as responsible for poverty-related issues, and as responding to or expected to respond to it. However, the UK government, as well as business, also featured significantly as responsible parties. Partly as a reflection of this, and of the thematic focus upon politics and the economy more generally, political voices were the most regularly cited sources in the coverage of poverty. Business sources also featured strongly. Although citizens' perspectives, including those directly affected by poverty, were often featured, there was a significant gender bias here. As for sourcing overall, female voices were very greatly outnumbered by male – a notable feature of the coverage in terms of its representativeness.

In the next chapter we turn to examine the factors conditioning the production of poverty news. Drawing upon extensive interview research, we examine the practices, experiences and challenges for journalists and editors, analysing how they reflected upon poverty and poverty reporting in Wales.

Notes

1 Totals are more than 100% because more than one 'experience of poverty' was identified within each news item.

2 This category included specific references to government budget cuts or austerity measures (at local authority, WG, UK national government, EU and third sector levels) for example because the anticipated losses of investment funds due to Brexit would leave communities poorer or threaten jobs.

3 This category was coded when the notion of 'worklessness' was specifically referred to, as for example in the expression 'cultures of worklessness'.

4 The category 'structural' was used when the implied structural cause of poverty referred to general economic pressures or trends in some way more generally, pressures emanating from rising costs of living or just 'the way things are' economically and when there was no explicit connection of these pressures to the economy in Wales.

5 The total number (n=) is greater here than the total number of news items in the sample (n=1498) because all 'consequences' of poverty mentioned within each story were coded.

6 Includes explicit references to 'social exclusion' combined with a category coded as 'opportunities', which included references to lack of opportunities to access secure or well-paying jobs, apprenticeships or more general references to a lack of future options to improve one's life, and also category coded as 'low attainment', which included stories which used this term explicitly with a more general social meaning than attainment in education.

7 New tax raising powers for the Welsh Government were introduced in April 2019, allowing ministers in Wales to raise income tax by up to 10p in every £1 for each band. However, the current administration has pledged not to raise income tax rates before the next Assembly election in 2021.

CHAPTER 4

Journalistic Experiences of Reporting Poverty

Introduction

Our interview research involved talking to 19 journalists and editors working in English- and Welsh- language news across broadcast, print and online media in a variety of news organisations in Wales. Each of our participants were asked about their journalistic values and experiences of reporting on poverty, how they understood and rated its newsworthiness as a topic, the opportunities, challenges and pressures that they had faced in reporting on these issues and their engagement with the third sector in this work.

A thematic analysis of the interviews follows, providing an insight into the perspectives on of news media professionals working in Wales. The findings are organised into three main sections: Poverty and Its Newsworthiness, Representation and Diversity, and Reporting Challenges and Experiences with the Third Sector.

Poverty and its newsworthiness

Understandings of poverty

Journalists talked about their understanding of poverty in different ways, citing official definitions and statistics, but most often emphasising the human and personal experiences through which they felt the meaning of poverty was most strikingly conveyed. Some of these accounts highlighted experiences of people unable to meet their basic living costs. For example:

> it's living below a certain standard and … struggling to make ends meet essentially isn't it? You know, a lot of people don't live in comfort, they

How to cite this book chapter:
Moore, K. 2020. *Reporting on Poverty: News Media Narratives and Third Sector Communications in Wales.* Pp. 53–75. Cardiff: Cardiff University Press. DOI: https://doi.org/10.18573/book4.d. License: CC-BY-NC-ND 4.0

don't have the money to pay all their bills, struggling to feed the kids or themselves ... I think that, for me, is poverty: when you can't afford to pay all your bills and have some standard of living as well. (Print news editor, English language)

I suppose it's people who are struggling to make ends meet on a regular basis and might have to go without meals or might have to have second-hand clothes for their kids all that kind of thing. They might have to forego some of life's luxuries, something simple like a trip to the pub, order a takeaway, but we might take for granted – it doesn't happen for those families ... people might assume that it's people going to soup kitchens or living on the streets, but actually poverty ... people are living on that scale as well. (Online news editor, English language)

Poverty was also depicted as a more complex issue, and one that is not always visible. They connected poverty with everyday struggles and managing the pressures of contemporary life, with accessing social opportunities, with powerlessness and restricted hopes for the future, and with high stakes decision-making in the face of financial difficulties:

Poverty used to mean you didn't have enough money, so you couldn't buy anything, whereas the rise of free available credit means that now, being poor, you know ... it's not about being poor in terms of disposable income anymore really, because you can have a credit card, you might have been able to provide really nice trainers ... clothes, for your child, but it's because you've got ten thousand pounds on a credit card ... That's a completely different type of poverty, it's much less recognisable in terms of ... the stereotypes ... you know, raggedy clothes and ... not being able to eat and that kind of thing. (Print/online news editor)

The statistical definition would be, percentage of people living below the poverty line, but I don't think that's how we look at poverty in terms of the way we cover it. It's people who, for us, use food banks, struggle to pay their bills ... have limited access to technology and opportunities that other people do. I think that's kind of how we look at it, because that's how families think about it, so it's families who are struggling to pay food and bills and can't send their children on school trips because they can't afford to pay for them, and you know, the cost of school uniform. We try to look at poverty from that perspective rather than the statistical one because I don't know that that tells our listeners anything. (Radio news editor)

Someone who doesn't have enough money to look after themselves and their family ... comfortably even, but in an acceptable way, you know? To keep warm, food, clothes, to keep looking smart too so that someone can move on in society, in education, to do what they want in life. (Radio journalist)

To me personally, it's related to the family situation where there are families that are doing everything within their ability to do the best for their children etc. but that are still behind with their rent and behind with payments, and can't go on holiday and can't buy school uniform and new trainers etc. Where people are trying their best to do the best for themselves, whereas you have families on probably the same income but who spend it unequally within the family – that the children are suffering for them to have a flat screen television and you know a night in the pub, or whatever it is. (Online news producer, Welsh language)

Human experiences were a central focus in journalistic reflections upon the meaning of poverty and how it should be covered. Indeed, interviewees reflected thoughtfully on the nature of poverty *as* news in their accounts. Many expressed the belief that public understandings of poverty in Wales were likely to be out of step with its reality across the country and limited in terms of the policies pursued to address it. They reflected how, in part at least, limitations in public understanding might be connected to the nature of, and possible gaps in, the news coverage of poverty. Concerns widely expressed included the notion that acknowledging poverty stories exist close to home is a fundamentally uncomfortable idea. As one Welsh-language broadcast reporter told us, 'I don't think that the audience want to hear about these'. In such accounts, the newsworthiness of poverty could be seen as a matter of 'whether or not there's an appetite for it from readers' (Print Journalist, English Language). Furthermore, as one radio journalist explained, in an environment where a multitude of subjects and issues compete for space on news agendas, poverty news could be squeezed out: 'there are different stories pushing the news agenda than there was fifteen, ten years ago'. By contrast, other journalists felt that poverty issues are now *more* newsworthy, with one print editor asserting, 'poverty is far higher up the news agenda than it's probably ever been in my experience'.

Factors influencing newsworthiness

The key factors thought to influence poverty's newsworthiness were all figured as bringing a 'new angle' to the coverage. These included newly relevant content, such as stories about the digital exclusion of vulnerable groups such as the elderly missing out on online banking benefits and payment discounts. As exemplified by the following reflections by news editors upon the coverage of child poverty, most journalists highlighted the importance of a 'new angle':

Because Wales is a poor country you get quite a lot of stories about poverty and child poverty in particular and suppose we ask ourselves the question, 'Okay, what is new in this piece of research or in this press release?' So you can tell something you haven't told them before. It's a news program and they do tend to find that the stories come around very regularly, so you kind of ask the question, 'What is different about it? What are we going to see or hear about this story in particular?' (Broadcast news editor)

There are certain things you can absolutely pinpoint that will make a good story: it's got to have a news 'hook' to it, it's got to have some new research or some new figures, or a strong line into it. A report looking at child poverty in Wales has a very general top line to it – how do we get into that, I need to be sold by a line to say 'this report has found that...' and it doesn't need to be statistics, that's a very obvious one, when charities do a bit of research and come up with some good statistics for us to kind of quantify the problem. But it can also just be ... they've managed to get a fairly high profile figure on board to have a strong statement about something, to call for action, or they've launched a new service, so it has to have something new about it. It can't just be a rehashing of something I feel like I've heard a lot before. I'm always looking for something new, a reason for doing something. (Broadcast news editor)

According to those we interviewed, the placement of a poverty story and whether or not it is profiled prominently depends on a number of factors, which vary according to the type of news outlet. Most journalists mentioned the idea of 'meaningfulness' to their specific audiences. For example, for local papers, 'meaningfulness' might be whether it is a 'town-wide' issue affecting many people in an area, and for regional or nationally targeted media a more quantified sense of 'how much of an audience it would resonate with' (print/online editor, English language). Indeed, thinking about a story's resonance with target audiences was at the centre of many journalists' understanding of newsworthiness:

It may be a story about Food Bank use in North Wales ... it may be on [Regional Outlet] we'd run that quite high up, because it's a family orientated station where we're sort of looking to speak to Mums as it being a female skewed station. The person who's doing that bulletin will decide. (Broadcast journalist, English language)

We know that Wales is very different to other parts of the UK in lots of different ways, certainly when it comes to areas in deprivation and poverty, class, for example. So we would want to reflect the portrayal here in Wales ... For us it's the Welsh agenda that dominates – the Welsher the better for us! (Television news editor, English language)

Similarly, some journalists working in radio in the Welsh language felt newsworthiness was signalled when stories generated a significant reaction from their audience, with those about Wales and the Welsh language most likely to do this. In online news, news value judgements could be much more 'live' and responsive, the placement of a story changing depending on its hits, as one Welsh-language producer explained:

> Say that we put a story on – the re-opening of Llanwern Steel works or something – the second slot at seven o'clock in the morning, and that you see in the figures by nine that it's not gripping maybe, we will change it a little bit, tinker with it, move it to the fifth slot and stick something else instead of it, and see what happens, you know.

Others reflected more sceptically about this basis for the promotion or relegation of stories as a 'click based model for journalism', noting how it can be experienced as a pressure upon journalists with potentially damaging effects for the quality of news:

> People are aware that they are expected to produce material which is going to get clicks and they will do so, and I think that it does have an impact on the kind of content that is being produced. (Print reporter, English language)

However, the significance of potential illustrative techniques to represent the issues and engage audiences with a story also featured strongly in journalists' views on newsworthiness. For example, the placement of a story could be affected by the perceived 'strength' or credibility of a guest or sources informing it, both in terms of their first-hand perspective and in delivery, for example in live broadcast news. Stories seen as most successful were often those that profiled the experiences of ordinary people in order to highlight a wider socio-economic issue or problem:

> If you've got someone who's really got something to say … that is local, and then that's really got a good story behind it … that would go further forward every day for me. (Print news editor, English language)

As such, journalists working across print, broadcast and online media all said that incorporating case studies was a 'very powerful' way to engage audiences with stories about poverty. Whilst statistics and reports might provide a hook for those stories, representing human experiences and everyday realities made them much more meaningful, illustrating the relevance of the facts and figures in people's lives:

> The information which we need is to be able to communicate things through script such as facts and figures. Charities are very good with things like that. They provide things like media packs and things which give and provide information and reports which are precise and go into

more depth. But what is failing is that the examples do not illustrate anything – the people … To do a television programme on [eviction] we
either need to speak with someone who has been evicted from their home
or we need to film someone being evicted from their homes … because it
illustrates the situation – which is more powerful – seeing something happen and by illustrating something powerful it communicates the message
… to show the actual impact rather than saying that X is up 5% – by show-
ing it is stronger than the statistic. (Programme producer, Welsh language)

So, say there's been a slight drop in the number of children living below
the poverty line, right, and that's the, that's the press release … That
doesn't mean anything to anyone really, you know … it's an important
statistic for the Welsh Government to know, probably, but in terms of
getting your head around that as a reader, you've got nothing to compare it to … you don't see that in your, in your daily life. Whereas you
know, if you had a family who used to … not be able to do X, Y, Z, but
now … the circumstances have changed, now they can, then that's at
least slightly more meaningful to us to what it means to be below the
poverty line. (Print/online editor, English language)

Other journalists explained how reliable expert testimony could offer another
technique for enhancing the newsworthiness of a story. This was characteris-
tically the case in reporting less well recognised or established issues as, for
example, working households in poverty, as one editor explained:

That studio spot of an expert voice in the studio with your presenter,
especially if it's something when there is more to say, bits to unpick from
it and some other lines to go on, that's really useful to help as a storytelling tool. (Broadcast news editor, English language)

Asked to identify what they felt were the particularly 'big' or newsworthy stories
on poverty in Wales, many journalists talked about the EU referendum and/or
Brexit as events potentially shaping the economic and social conditions and
experiences of poverty in important ways. Other poverty stories mentioned as
significant, including industry, jobs and unemployment, and especially the fate
of the Tata Steel works in South Wales, also corresponded with the coverage
identified in our content study. However, journalists also mentioned a range
of other issues not necessarily so well reflected in the coverage we analysed,
including child poverty, food banks, vacant shops, policies to cut benefits,
housing inequality, education and pollution.

One key concern, with respect to accurately portraying important stories,
was how poverty, as a continuing and systemic issue, is not easily captured in
news. If it is always 'there' and therefore never entirely 'new' as such, when and
why poverty becomes a focus as 'news' carries potentially important consequences for public understandings of the issue. Some journalists highlighted

this as a key tension in terms of values: to offer an accurate picture of poverty could entail covering stories repeatedly, but with nothing very 'new' to report:

> With regards to poverty … it's something that's just there in the background, it's this residual, you know, social phenomenon that doesn't really change, it fluctuates in terms of levels of poverty, but really it's just constant, and because of the nature of news – which tends to cover things that are changing or new or developing – it can ignore some really important stories because they are – they were there yesterday, they'll be there tomorrow. (Print news editor, English language)

> Because it's an on-going issue, it's … we don't want to be going every six months, 'by the way, do you remember six months ago we told you that there are people living in poverty? Well, by the way, they still live in poverty today', without there being a new problem or a new solution to talk about. So, if something comes up which is a new scheme … that is being announced in the Valleys to try to target, you know, working families to help them with child care so that Mums can go back to work, something like that, well we'll talk about that, because that's a new angle on it, but if it's just some figures that show pretty much the same amount of people are living in poverty as they were last time we talked about it, it becomes really difficult for us to talk and keep that issue on the agenda, even though it's hugely important. (Radio journalist, English language)

> It does change with the news cycle to a degree, because I remember doing a lot of stories about mortgages and repossessions and, food banks for instance. We did a lot of stories … when the food banks started reappearing having not been something people talked about, but after a while you know we've had food banks for 3, 4 years and so there's a point where we think actually, 'what more can we say about food banks now'? You know, we feel we've explored that territory quite widely. So, it does change depending on the economic circumstances at the time. (Broadcast news editor, English language)

Less obvious in these accounts were reflections upon the type of coverage that we found most frequently in our content study – stories featuring poverty more incidentally and primarily focused upon other issues, such as politics or the economy. However, some journalists did touch upon the difficulties in representing meaningful connections between the macroeconomic or political actions that frequently provide the 'news hooks' for relevant stories, the implications of such forces in people's experiences of poverty and the recognition of these in the reality of people's lives:

> Unemployment, the budget, the European economic plans, a lot of reports come out about child poverty because of the Welsh Assembly's targets …

and perhaps reflecting these, I think, are the hardest ones do. It can be wishy-washy, what you mean about poverty ... people might not consider themselves poor, or live in poor areas. There's poverty everywhere but it's also hidden as well. (Broadcast news producer, Welsh language)

When we do cover stories like the Tata steel crisis by featuring the people that are so concerned about their jobs, to a degree what we are doing is highlighting the risk to them of economic inactivity. How they could spiral into quite a difficult economic position if they were to leave their job. So I think we actually reflect poverty in some cases when we don't even realise that we are doing it. (Broadcast news editor, English language)

Such stories also contribute to the news narrative on poverty in Wales in important ways, communicating ideas to audiences about the relative news value of poverty and its salience within the 'bigger picture' of the wider public agenda.

Representation and diversity

I think poverty is a major issue clearly in Wales and the social and economic landscape here means people tend to be less well off than in England for example. So it's important for us to reflect those stories. (Broadcast and digital editor)

Although the journalists and editors we interviewed expressed broadly similar values, ideas and aspirations about the reporting of poverty, these did not necessarily map neatly onto the range of opinions and perspectives they related about what reporting looks like in practice. One key ideal was that reporting should fairly represent the extent and range of opinions and experiences across the diverse communities of Wales. A concern to represent that diversity accurately was widespread amongst journalists and editors whether working in print, online and broadcast, commercial or publicly funded media.

Some strongly emphasised representing diversity as a duty that should be embedded within organisational culture. Whilst for broadcasters this may be conditioned by public service remits, diversity was clearly recognised as a responsibility:

You need to do that, [it's] the role of a publicly funded broadcaster or news organisation ... We have specialists and we'd expect all of them to ... to bring diversity on screen as part of their brief and have the contact with diverse communities as part of the brief to know who to speak to about poverty as part of their brief. (Broadcast producer)

However, a lack of diversity within the profession was frequently noted with concern about the structural impediments in recruitment, how 'diversity' is understood and how journalists' backgrounds may impact how poverty stories are represented:

> We need to work on the kinds of people we employ internally, because we don't naturally have those contacts, necessarily, if we're not employing the right people here. There is work to do there, so some of that responsibility lies with us. (Broadcast editor, English language)

> The nature of people who get into broadcast journalism now ... they're probably gonna come from better off backgrounds than they did 30 years ago ... and a more educated background and if you have to ultimately pay for your undergraduate course and then pay the fees ... for a year of postgraduate study before I can then get a job (particularly in newspapers) ... or to be one of the many thousands of people who want to go work in broadcasting, that's really, really tough to do if you come from a deprived background yourself. (Broadcast producer/editor, English language)

> When we talk about diversity, quite often we talk about ethnicity, we talk about age, we talk about gender, we talk about sexuality, religion etc. which is all great, everybody's equal. But how often do we talk about whether we come from a working class background or whether we come from a very affluent type background? Where our parents worked in factories or struggled to work, or, you know, lived on, you know, social or whatever, or whether our parents were solicitors and, you know, doctors – and how often we don't really have those conversations ... and I think we suffer from that, I think we really do. (Broadcast news correspondent, English language)

> As a lot of people who have worked within the media and the press are middle classes ... they write and do programmes about things which they already know about ... whereas of course we need to do more about people from different communities ... such as poor people who have social issues and we need to do more about programmes about things like that. (Broadcast producer, Welsh language)

Some journalists did not believe that poverty was any more neglected than any other story. However, others believed that experiences of poverty really were not reported as often as they should be, with some demographic groups, including Muslim communities, black and minority ethnic communities (BAME) and refugees felt to be especially under-represented in poverty news:

> In Wales ... we are used to linguistic arguments and all sorts of things like that, but also there are whole communities of people from ethnic backgrounds too that don't get attention. Things are changing slightly by now, but that is also something that has been ignored over the years,

and now that it's such an argument, people are starting to wake up and think 'Well, what is happening in the community?' (Print news editor)

Many journalists reflected that the experiences of particularly vulnerable groups (especially children) might also be under-represented in poverty coverage, in part due to additional ethical considerations and potential difficulties in featuring them:

> Clearly if you are a 13 year old child ... living in poverty, then your parents might say okay that's fine for you to go on the telly and tell your story, that's fine. But then we have to consider as well things around that: that child might have to go to school following day and be bullied because they are poor or can't afford to do things, and that's an issue we have to consider as well – to be ethically fair. (Broadcast news editor, English language)

> I think schools and education, people in those deprived areas, is something we don't see enough of. And children, case studies are hard enough but case studies when people talk about child poverty and what it means to be a child growing up in one of those households, do they have enough to eat and all those sorts of things, we just don't see that at all. (Broadcast editor, English language)

More than one journalist mentioned problems facing young people in poverty, including drug abuse and suicide, as stories that tended to be 'untold' due to challenges in gaining ethical consent and access to case study participants:

> People under 16 are very difficult to ... get permission to interview them, for acceptable and important reasons. But I know a crew of young girls in the area where I live that take methadone often and steal, and their lives are in pieces, and they are 13/14 years old. And it seems that there's nobody there ... with the time or energy to help them, whether parents or teacher or whatever. I'm not saying for a second that it's the teacher's fault, but I think there's a problem with drugs and young people, and it's very hard to tell that story because of their age. You will never get their parent's permission, it's hard to get over that. (Broadcast journalist, English language)

> The scale of drug abuse probably in the Valleys is probably quite high ... possibly the scale of suicide maybe amongst young people ... I think it's fair to say it's quite concerning because people just don't feel that they've got ... adequate lives, fulfilling lives ... it's really sad how we've sort of got into this position ... you need a case study of somebody who's going through that in order to be able to explain it, and ... unless you can

get that it's incredibly difficult story to tell. (Broadcast correspondent, English language)

Another key group felt to be under-represented included those living in rural areas in Wales, in part because of the perceived reluctance of people from small communities to talk about the difficulties they faced. Such problems accessing rural stories were thought exacerbated by the location of media organisations (and therefore most journalists) in Cardiff and other big urban areas:

There can also be individuals who live in poor areas of Britain or Wales who do not have the media attention ... I mean if we look at the Valleys especially and rural areas of Wales, the media does not reach out that far and the newspapers are also in Cardiff – slightly more in the West and a little to the North but not much in the centre of Wales ... there are not people there to do the stories ... also the share of communities who are ready to share their stories and experiences, like Muslims, the elderly perhaps, people perhaps who are shy ... they are not as accessible. (Broadcast producer, Welsh language)

Geographically it can be very difficult to cover rural poverty ... we very often can't send a reporter to Pembrokeshire to speak to one person about their experiences of poverty, because it's too time consuming. So, we have one reporter who's based in South Wales, and you can't always justify that amount of time to speak to one person, because you've then got to try and put the rest of the package together, and that could take up to a whole day working on one story, which for us, logistically we can't do. So rural poverty is one that I think we struggle to cover ... we very often ask people to do interviews by iPhone. So we'll call them up, they'll record their comments on their phone, their smart phone, and send them back to us, and we use that audio on air then. By the nature of poverty, people (the case studies) we try to contact – don't often have access to that technology, and if they do they're concerned about whether it will cost them to send us emails ... 'Have you got Skype?' 'Well no, we haven't got broadband because we can't afford it.' I know that's a generalisation, but that's quite difficult sometimes in getting the case studies, but it's something we would like a little bit more of. (Radio journalist, English language)

Both print and broadcast news journalists suggested that the demographics of target audiences might play a part in the kinds of groups best served by news output. Whilst Wales-focused news was clearly paramount and mentioned often by journalists, for regional and local media the 'relevance' of content was also conditioned by the perceived concerns of particular, geographically based target audiences. To this end, journalists spoke of the investment of some news organisations in specialist and area-based correspondents (e.g. a 'Valleys correspondent') to serve their 'heartland audience'. This, they told us, facilitated regular newsworthy stories with coverage: it is 'more successful when you've actually got somebody living on the patch and working on the patch' (broadcast news producer/editor, English language).

Other demographic factors, such as gender and age were also acknowledged to play a part in the coverage journalists expected to produce, depending on the target audience of particular channels:

> I think we are much better at representing older people and their issues and problems because our programme is generally skewed towards the 55 and over audience. (Online editor, English language)

Others explained how the typical demographic of target audiences, by contrast, might be relatively affluent with interest in poverty driven by attention to social or policy issues rather than direct experiences of poverty:

> People from higher social classes and ... people who are active in civil society ... who are going to be more interested perhaps in the kind of statistical or statistically based stories, even than the people themselves who are affected by the poverty. (Print news reporter, English language)

Finally, the challenge of producing representative coverage was felt particularly intensely by those working in Welsh-medium news. Interviewees highlighted the 'scarcity' of Welsh speakers exacerbating the challenges generally facing journalists:

> It makes our work difficult sometimes when you want to do a story but there are no Welsh speakers involved ... In the valleys for instance, that's been a real problem for us because not a lot of Welsh is spoken there. Perhaps we don't do enough in these deprived communities because of the scarcity of Welsh. (Broadcast reporter, Welsh language)

> There is a large percentage of Welsh speaking individuals who are middle class you know. It is then as hard as ever to get examples of people from different communities to speak out about their issues. (Programme producer, Welsh language)

> When charities contact us, saying, 'Oh I've raised ... drew your attention to this particular story about poverty', and then you say 'Oh, have you got someone to go and talk?' 'Oh no, I didn't think of that, Oh so and so will do it' 'No, he/she doesn't speak Welsh', 'Oh, Welsh? O dear, erm...' and then all that awareness comes in to things then you know? There was a time they didn't cater for the Welsh language, they didn't even think about Welsh when sending statements and when preparing

resources beforehand. But, by now, the situation has improved a lot. (Online producer, Welsh language)

The discussions surrounding these challenges in representing diversity often developed into reflections which further contextualised issues concerning journalists in their work on poverty, how these issues were addressed or overcome and how relationships with the third sector played into journalists' practice.

Reporting challenges and experiences with the third sector

Another key focus of our interviews was the expectations that journalists and those responsible for third sector communications on poverty hold about one another's roles in the production of news. In particular, we were interested in exploring how the possibilities and challenges of one another's practice are understood, how these ideas play a part in working relationships and in how poverty news is ultimately reported. This section focuses upon the views of journalists and editors, whilst the perspectives of third sector communications practitioners will be explored in the final section of Chapter 4.

All journalists interviewed experienced third sector communications in some form as part of their work reporting poverty. For some, this predominantly involved receiving press releases or other contact from NGOs. However, for others, proactively contacting third sector organisations, either regularly or occasionally, was a feature of their practice.

Across journalists' accounts, both positive and negative assumptions about, and experiences of engaging with, third sector organisations were a feature. However, overall, a general sense of goodwill and openness towards engaging with the third sector remained a clear common theme. This was evident from accounts expressing an aspiration for more effective engagement with charities and third sector organisations. Many journalists also expressed a belief that the third sector endeavours to understand journalists' needs, and tries to offer ideas for stories that they imagine will be useful:

> A press officer at a certain charity can change and, actually, that can make a huge difference because you know, the press officers who 'get' the picture thing and understand the quick turnaround, and even the ones you phone up with short notice request and say 'we're doing this story, any chance you can help' and you know that they will genuinely go out there an help, that makes a big difference. (Broadcast editor, English language)

This does not necessarily mean, however, that engagements with the third sector were always seen as productive. Indeed, journalists identified a number of issues relating to the *relevance* of the information offered to them as well variations in its timeliness, quality and specificity as important factors.

Most journalists referred to working to tight timescales as part of the nature of the job of news production. Many noted the increasingly limited resources with which to meet these demands. Whilst some news organisations maintained reporters responsible for business or economic issues, many did not have specialist social affairs correspondents with a remit dedicated to reporting on poverty issues or a 'patch' where stories about poverty might be frequently anticipated:

> As far as I'm concerned, someone decided that only this and this amount of money we have for reporters and these are the four or five most important jobs ... So it's [reporting poverty is] a job for everyone really, to bring the stories here and highlight interesting things. (Radio journalist, English language)

> I don't think it's localised anymore, that local link is gone ... most of the stories that come ... are done from Cardiff by journalists who, yeah, do decent enough stories, but are far as far as the locals are concerned ... they don't know who they are, never heard of them before, never seen them, they don't live round there ... the local man or the local woman doesn't ... exist. (Broadcast correspondent, English language)

> I think what we're not getting is the raw examples of, 'this is what poverty looks like' because the ... grassroots level of community journalism is not having the contact with people that it's had. (Broadcast series producer, English language)

More generally, as newsrooms employ fewer people than in the past, many journalists are required to do more: be multiskilled, work faster and carry out a greater range of roles in the end-to-end production of content. These pressures, some argue, have increasingly bound journalists to their desks, reliant on sources of information easily accessible online, such that, as one print journalists told us, 'in the main, people do not go out'. These pressures have also, some argue, increased the influence and uncritical reproduction of public relations content in journalism, or 'churnalism' (Davies, 2011). Some journalists expressed concern about trends towards more 'office-based' roles for journalists, which distanced them from the 'real' experiences of people. Other journalists lamented the loss of 'traditional' in favour of more 'blogger-type roles', and expressed concern that 'there are not many of us who do the most serious stuff these days' (print journalist, English language).

In connection with these trends, there were some differences between how journalists talked about press releases from the third sector and their role in news making. Whilst press releases were widely accepted and generally valued, some journalists, especially those working in current affairs rather than news, insisted that getting 'out there' themselves remained crucial, with press releases being, at best, marginal to their practice.

Many journalists mentioned the abundance of press releases received by news organisations, reflecting upon the consequences of their centrality in journalism:

> What they are doing is republishing press releases. So, perversely, the NGO voice – I think is probably stronger, because they are filling the void of organised information in a way that social media isn't because it's non-filtered and the community journalism isn't, because it's no longer there. (Broadcast series producer, English language)

In view of the time pressures facing journalists, some placed the onus upon press officers to deliver reliable, verified and/or clear information:

> The reports usually contain detailed statistics which are sourced ... one assumes that they will have been fact checked before the reports have been released ... It would be a pretty sad indictment a third sector organization or a charity if they were producing reports based on dodgy statistics ... I think that there is an in-built assumption that when you get a report from a body that has a some status and that has respect, that the statistics that it produces and uses in the report ... to arrive at certain conclusion will be accurate ... You do not have the time to fact check those statistics so you will take that on trust. (Print journalist, English language)

> It's always handy when there's a press release which is sent through and it kind of breaks down for you the key statistics. Sometimes you'll get sent information which is just reams and reams of tables and charts so you have to think for you're pitching this story to – that is a bunch of people in the newsroom who are very busy, who have to make quite quick decisions about things. If it's not quite clearly laid out for you with a clear top line to the story then it will just get lost. This sounds a bit lazy, but if you're asking people to go through that kind of information in that kind of depth then they probably won't because quick decisions to have to be made, but if there's a clear headline to the story and some key facts to flesh around ... that's useful. (Online editor, English language)

Others advocated a more open view towards less polished press releases in some circumstances, emphasising their potential value as raw source material:

> As long as it's engaging ... then great you know, we will re-work it. Sometimes, you get press releases and it's just not worth the work you've got to put in to it. You know, to get it up to the standard that you want ..., it's a fine line isn't it, you've got to sort of look at it sometimes and even though they're not a big organisation, they won't be as 'press releasy' ...

sometimes the smaller ones can be better because they're not as structured ... and they're trying to get this point across which you know, sometimes is better than the bigger organisation. (Print journalist/ editor, English language)

However, others expressed greater frustration about the quality of information in some press releases, varying levels of expertise amongst press officers and their understanding of journalistic needs:

> The problem is, of course, is that there's plenty of charities that exist nowadays and ... these reports are constant. I don't know where these people get time to write all of the reports! And then, a lot of these reports fall between two chairs and don't get attention. And maybe people then go ... 'Oh poverty, not again!' Press releases make me very, very angry because it surprises me so many of them that arrive and people can't write, and that can't draw attention in the opening paragraph ... they can't find the news line in their own reports. (Online producer, Welsh language)

> There's a wide range – some press releases are better than others. The expertise is there if you question them. They think that once they have sent the press release that is it. They don't understand that there is more for them to do and to provide. They need a better understanding of our demands and requirements. You will find that if a journalist goes to work for them then we see a huge difference in the help we get and the access we get. (Broadcast producer, Welsh language)

Whilst writing quality and the clarity of the 'top line' was clearly a key issue, other elements concerning the relevance and specificity of information also arose in discussions. The specificity of facts and figures to Wales, rather than the UK as a whole in press releases was identified as crucial, yet often lacking or inadequate:

> One thing that happens quite a lot I would say, which for me makes it tricky to do, is quite often charities will have both a Welsh and a UK/ British [office] and will do some statistical research, but it will be a UK wide survey. Then they extrapolate Welsh figures from that, and when you look at it, actually, the sample size for Wales is so tiny! ... So then, to make it feel like a bona fide Welsh story, you are talking about research which is based on such a small sample it then becomes tricky ... You question the quality of the research ... and maybe not emphasise that part of the story and try and think of something else, because it wouldn't be right to go on a big kind of headline ... I think that's something, understandably, charities do quite a lot because, obviously, it's expensive to do research. (Television news editor, English language)

Another frustration highlighted was a perceived lack of responsiveness on the part of third sector organisations in supporting the development of stories they had themselves brought to the attention of journalists:

> One thing I would say, which sounds ridiculous but does happen a surprising amount, is stories embargoed to a certain day when people aren't available. So you want to do the story, and you phone and they say, 'I'm sorry they're not available that day!' You'd be surprised how often that happens. Or the case study isn't available on that day. So they want you to film that on a different day, and actually it's really hard to do all that. So all those things will make it harder and harder to get that piece on because then it becomes a massive juggle. (Broadcast editor, English language)

> Fairly regularly, more than you'd expect ... press releases come in, we speak to the organisation, and they don't have anybody available to speak to us on the day they've sent out that press release, or on the day the press release is embargoed for, or they don't know about case studies, or they've thought about case studies but they'll go away and make phone calls. Fairly regularly we see stories die a death because actually the organisation – that's probably spent many thousands of pounds and maybe many weeks, maybe even many months, on a story idea, on a publicity push – then can't actually deliver on the day. (Broadcast producer, English language)

On the other hand, some journalists acknowledged that when they did contact charities it could be rather 'last minute', making challenging or unrealistic demands upon organisations to produce useful information:

> Yeah, yeah that's fair enough. I'm not sure what the answer is to this, other than being able to double the budgets on programmes, which isn't going to happen anytime soon! (Broadcast journalist, English language)

> [Laughs] I'm sure that I have ... somewhere down all of the years. I find that ... it's hard, and I know before I do that phone call that I'm hedging my bets massively. (Online producer, Welsh language)

> I think from their perspective it is last minute. From our perspective, we pretty much call up as soon as we get a story, so it's not last minute. In our perspective, it's just that our deadlines are very, very short, certainly for broadcast, and social media has made that even shorter. So, if figures are published like, say, Welsh Government provides some new figures on something related to poverty, those will come out in the morning. We'll see politicians, we'll start talking about them, charities will start

talking about them on social media and then that will filter through to our audience by the afternoon, and if we're not coming to that story on air the next day people are going, 'Oh, I already saw that on Facebook, I've already read an article about that yesterday!' So social media has made that process a lot quicker and I would say as soon as we get an email or we see a story we'll contact the charity we want to speak to straight away. The deadline for us is usually sort of the end of that day, so very often they will only have about three or four hours or something like that, to get together. (Broadcast journalist, English language)

Accessibility, timeliness and cooperation in developing stories were themes frequently mentioned with reference to case studies. Case studies were identified as 'absolutely vital' (Broadcast news editor, English language), without which stories considered generally more difficult and less likely to find space on news agendas:

More often than not ... we would be looking for a case study, because at the end of the day, we're in the business of telling stories. So, you need people's stories to tell. That's the only way, really, that you really get the message across and it's far more powerful to hear a story from the horse's mouth (Broadcast news editor, English language)

To have a fresh voice and a fresh perspective ... of someone who was affected – that's always what we want from a story, but we recognise what we want from this topic – you can't always get that. But if there was a case study offered on that kind of story, we would be more likely to take it. (Broadcast journalist/producer, English language)

The third sector's role in facilitating meetings with potential case study subjects was widely identified by journalists as very useful. As already discussed, there was widespread concern that 'raw examples' of poverty could be overlooked because journalists do not have sufficient contact with people in their communities or at the 'grass roots'. The value of talking face to face with people was raised repeatedly – especially access facilitated by regular contacts in charities or think tanks whose expertise on poverty and communication skills were trusted and respected:

I did a programme a few years ago on young people coming out of prison and there was a young woman from an ethnic background in Cardiff. She came in to the studio to talk about the experience of being sent to prison in her teens. And she got the opportunity to point her finger at someone else in the studio that was in power, or in a situation to do something to stop the cycle of breaking the law amongst young people that come from poor backgrounds, or that have various problems. And that politician's answer was that there's a need to be tougher ... and her reaction was, 'No you need to stop and listen to people like me', and it was very effective ... The example was just fantastic, it was very powerful. (Broadcast news editor)

The importance of exclusivity of access to case study participants was also high-lighted, with journalists favouring specific examples chosen for different pro-grammes, even within the same news organisation:

> I'd certainly say in terms of case studies, we would much prefer to have a case study that is only offered to our programme. If we know that that person has spoken to lots of outlets it sometimes feels that the story has already been told so we do like to be able to say, we like to know that the story is being told for the first time on our programmes. You'll often see, you know, one person being put up for interview for all media outlets ... that story, it may have been running all day. The person's story has been told already. So, what are we really offering the audience that's new on this particular story? That may be a bit off-putting. (Television news editor, English language)

The value of third sector contacts understanding such journalistic priorities was regularly acknowledged.

Journalists also talked about contacting charities proactively for useful con-tent. This was especially the case in Welsh-medium news and/or when spe-cific challenges were faced, such as producing stories about issues and contexts overseas. However, some journalists cautioned that regular contacts based on trusted relationships could also mean that the 'same voices' were heard, poten-tially impacting the breadth of ideas and experiences featured in their coverage. The importance of maintaining independence from third sector organisations in the interests of journalistic relevance and quality was also noted, not least in terms of the selection and assessment of case study examples:

> I'd want our news desks or planners to speak to them so you've got a real understanding of who that person is. Are they the right person for the story? Inevitably, charities – particularly if charities are pushing us a particular story – they might have somebody who fits their purposes or, (I'm sure they're just as busy as we are in terms of sort of media activi-ties) so they might just give us the first person that they come across, or may be the only person that they've got: they're trying to get the story on air, so that person will 'do'. I want journalistically to do something, which is our own journalism – to understand actually who the person is, what's the story they're telling? Is the story true? Does it actually fit in with what we understand as being the wider issue? (Broadcast editor/ producer, English language)

Indeed, whilst the role of charities as facilitators of case studies was widely recognised, many journalists emphasised a preference for working with people directly on potential stories, valuing the opportunity to use their journalistic skills more freely to access sources and develop examples without interventions from gatekeeper organisations:

> I think you get a more honest picture with journalism if you go out and get it yourself. (Online/print editor, English language)

> There's a feeling that if we went through the charities they would interfere too much or try to be too careful about what we can do … We feel that we are acting responsibly, but I'm sure they think differently. That can be very frustrating when we do things with adults and we think we are being professional without the need for anyone else's interference. (Broadcast news reporter, Welsh language)

> Our emphasis journalistically would be on finding these people for them to be able to give their evidence directly to us, rather than depend on other people, press officers or whatever or people that are a part of the charities to question people for us to be able to publish something. We'd tend not to do that, we'd rather question those people ourselves, because by questioning something raises, you can go after that question again and get a different colour or a more original and more loyal … to our journalism. (Print editor, Welsh language)

> We needed something on alcoholism and homelessness and we got into contact with one charity who work in the South and they said that they had three Welsh speakers and they said that they would ask the individuals and the answer was no … and that happens regularly … and that it is it … we could have met with the individuals first but no was the answer for that question also, so it is really hard … to know what the efforts are … I am not questioning their efforts but if they just asked via email then it is easy to say no to that, whereas if we met face to face and spent half an hour discussing … if you are going to go and meet someone then you can talk to them about the programme, and they say no … but they still want to do the programme and that is what we want to hear from the individual … we can get a lot of information from the individuals just by talking to them – not information to be used on the television but information which creates more of a story in our own minds as we have had access to speak directly with the individuals with case studies. (Programme producer, Welsh language)

A keen awareness of poverty as a potentially very sensitive issue to cover was very evident in many journalists' accounts. This applied especially in reflections upon featuring direct experiences of poverty and case studies of the impact of deprivation in people's lives. Journalists talked about difficulties in securing first-hand accounts due to a reluctance to trust journalists to handle their stories well. They also reflected upon other barriers, including the social stigma attached to poverty, people's feelings of shame at their circumstances, fear of public retribution for claiming welfare benefits and even of government sanction for speaking out about their circumstances:

> I think we're all aware of problems – particularly with stories on poverty case studies because obviously often don't, who are in that situation, they're sort of embarrassed by it and they don't want to go on the TV and talk about it. (Broadcast news editor, English language)

> Families that are trying their best but that are finding it hard, and that they're too proud to share the story … they are people who are just, through misfortune in the situation that they're in, and because they are proudly Welsh, they wouldn't want to share their story here. (Broadcast producer, Welsh language)

> You might want to … speak to someone who is directly affected by some of these cuts and … you may have the statistical information and you may want to put flesh on the bones by speaking to somebody who is affected. That can be more problematic and more difficult, partly because there are a lot of people – although they are affected by decisions that are taken – do not want to put their heads above the parapet … Sometimes it is a pride thing – that they do not want to be portrayed as some kind of victim, but I think also there is the fear some people have that if they do put their heads above the parapet, and they are claiming benefits, then they are going to be targeted and to have benefits taken off them … so that can be a problem. (Print news journalist, English language)

> When we do food bank stories we'll always ask if they, if some of their regular customers, so to speak, will have a chat with us … and very often people don't want to talk about it. So groups like that are very difficult to reach because they … don't want to talk about why they're using them, because they feel there is a stigma that, you know, maybe they're not providing for their family or the sort of tabloid stigma of, 'they are scroungers and claiming benefits'. They don't want to open themselves up, they're a bit scared of us in some respects, because of the impact of 'Benefit Street' … I think people are a little bit scared of talking about their experiences of it, and being open. (Broadcast journalist/producer, English language)

However, other journalists were keen to emphasise how such sensitivities could be mitigated, through employing certain techniques in reporting. They also stressed the importance of such approaches in order to include coverage of the most vulnerable groups:

> We've got lots of different ways now of doing interviews anonymously, it's quite common now for us to use reconstruction. We quite often film people's shadows instead of their faces, we'll often get actors to voice up people's voices if they want to be completely anonymous. So, we really do try to tackle the problems that come with sensitive stories like child protection. (Broadcast news editor, English language)

Indeed, overcoming the reluctance of potential case study participants was an issue upon which several journalists thoughtfully reflected:

> I am aware ... we persuade individuals to take part in programmes for a lot of reasons and I am not saying that journalists ... but the pressure is there to get the story and to get an example. Naturally, sometimes it is going to be like some sort of battle. (Broadcast producer, Welsh language)

> You have to find why they would want to take part in a programme ... and that is our job as journalists ... to explain to them ... It is very likely that they are going to say no but if you talk to them about what happened and then, well, one reason may be that by sharing the reason that perhaps their story might help other people ... This then helps them to take part and in actual fact they might help ten other people which is precious for the individual concerned ... and they live in the hope that their loss and their pain will help other people. (Broadcast producer, Welsh language)

Such reflections by journalists clearly demonstrate an awareness of the interests of individuals participating in case studies. However, they also highlight how journalistic priorities might focus upon finding a way to align those interests with those of the story.

Journalistic experiences: a summary

The similarities and differences between the ideas and approaches outlined in our interviews with journalists are not just characteristic of the reporting of poverty in their specific news contexts, but also more generally reflect professional ideals and values, differing routines, cultures and challenges in contemporary journalistic practice. The news professionals we interviewed were drawn from a cross-section of news organisations, working in English, in Welsh and bilingually, with ideas and beliefs conditioned by their particular experiences and the particular demands of their roles. Overall, our respondents were highly aware of the social significance of the ideas 'out there' on poverty and the potential contribution of news and current affairs to those ideas, the importance of fairly representing the range of experiences of poverty in Wales and of holding government policies and proposals to account. Clearly, however, there were a number of challenges thought to potentially limit the accuracy and meaningfulness of news coverage of poverty. These included the general difficulty of representing an ongoing issue 'as news' – a problem which (like climate change, for example) can lead to its marginalisation from news narratives, in spite of its ongoing salience and profound impacts upon people's lives. Rather than leading a story, poverty is often one detail, or subtext within a report – often focused on political or economic affairs – and may not be explicitly drawn out as a news angle. As such, meaningful shifts at the macro level may not always be well connected to the reality of people's livelihoods on the ground. Although a general consensus prevailed amongst interviewees that poverty is made most meaningful to audiences through exploring ordinary people's experiences, making this happen is clearly no small task in a fast-paced newsroom where resources feel stretched. Reflections upon the depletion of specialist and 'patch' correspondents suggested a dislocation between news professionals in the big cities and the lived realities of poverty in communities across the country. Similarly, the expertise required of journalists as generalists may have meant a loss of in-depth understanding of poverty, the meaningfulness of potential stories and further limitations to investigative work on the ground. Some journalists voiced concerns about how the lack of social diversity within the industry may further exacerbate such difficulties. Whereas current affairs journalists working to longer timescales spoke about their roles slightly differently, preferring to develop stories and cultivate the necessary relationships and understanding of the issues themselves, in news journalism a potentially problematic distance from the stories of ordinary people was evidently felt. Relationships with the third sector, to some degree, then, offered one means through which to reconnect journalists with poverty stories on the ground, providing in-depth information through reports and access to case studies from their front-line work with communities in Wales. Where understanding of the demands and challenges of news production were well understood by contacts in third sector organisations, such relationships were highly valued and talked about in terms of enhancing human interest reporting and the meaningful representation of poverty. However, journalists' accounts also suggested that such relationships came with tensions, and misapprehensions and could present impediments to quality reporting.

In the next chapter, we turn to the perspectives of third sector professionals reflecting upon their media communications practices on poverty, including their aims, experiences and challenges in engaging with the news media in Wales.

CHAPTER 5

Third Sector Experiences of Communicating Poverty

Introduction

Our interview research involved talking to 16 professionals working across a range of third sector organisations in Wales engaging with poverty in different ways. These included housing associations, homelessness charities, food banks, community and voluntary support organisations, equality advocacy organisations, religious groups and international NGOs. Whilst some of our participants worked in roles formally dedicated to, or responsible for, media communications, others engaged with media much more incidentally as part of their work. Each participant was asked about their views on news coverage of poverty, their own experiences and ideas about engaging with news media organisations and the opportunities, pressures and challenges faced in getting out their message on the issues that mattered to them. A thematic analysis of the interviews follows, providing an insight into the perspectives of third sector professionals working in Wales. The findings are organised into three main sections: Communication Aims and Expertise, Representation and Its Challenges and Relationships with the Media.

Communication aims and expertise

Our participants represented a range of organisations whose engagements with news media differed significantly in terms of regularity and directness. Some larger organisations employed personnel dedicated to handling public communications. These interviewees talked confidently about their communications work and strategic aims to influence policy and/or public opinion. Other organisations were more focused on the delivery of front-line services, directly

How to cite this book chapter:
Moore, K. 2020. *Reporting on Poverty: News Media Narratives and Third Sector Communications in Wales.* Pp. 77–107. Cardiff: Cardiff University Press. DOI: https://doi.org/10.18573/book4.e. License: CC-BY-NC-ND 4.0

supporting clients and/or seeking to influence policymakers more directly. As such, these organisations did not necessarily prioritise media communications or have roles for people exclusively responsible for it and tended to have less frequent contact with journalists.

Some interviewees had been journalists in their previous jobs and felt that this enabled them to bring to their roles an understanding of news media demands and pressures. This included how to produce effective press releases and sensitivity to the time and resource pressures faced by journalists:

> Having worked in the Welsh media ... I think they're all pretty fair and I think there's a good relationship there. I know their agenda – they want good stories, you know my agenda is to inform people, so we've got to play to their agenda by trying to write them in a way that will get into their papers. That perhaps means giving them a strong line ... or trying to find lots of case studies or things that they can follow up ... I understand the pressure they're under – in particular print journalism – and they haven't got the resources they once had and mistakes are inevitably made, and I think we're in an age when a lot of that's just got to be overlooked because we know how hard things are. (Advisor for communication/media officer)

Some reflected upon the differences between journalism and PR/communication roles highlighting issues such as professional expertise and values. For example, one media officer noted that how objectivity and balance are understood in a story could depend on the degree of in-depth knowledge of the issues a writer has – a perspective which also provided a counterpoint to some of the journalists' assumptions about the potentially negative influence of PR on the quality of journalism:

> When I was a reporter you could do ten different stories a day, whereas when you're in PR you're working, really, on one message through various different stories all the time ... which makes it for me much more satisfying because you develop a depth and a knowledge, and you get a chance to really understand the whole picture. And, it does show you how even hard, mature journalists think they know about a particular story, you realise, actually, 'you don't know the whole picture!' They're given one side for it, they think they know all the facts but you find that, actually, they don't know a lot. It's made me very suspicious of what I read in newspapers now as well. You think, 'there's another story there!' It's very difficult to write a story without being biased and without having an agenda and I think journalists may try to do that, but it's very, very difficult. (Advisor for communication/media officer)

Those in dedicated communications roles in the larger, national or international third sector organisations tended to have considerable experience working in public relations and/or the media. They described a combination of formal support structures and autonomy, which enabled them to plan ahead and carefully craft a tailored message for the Welsh audience as part of their everyday practice:

> They're basically a newsroom over in London ... so we get the UK draft of the press release, then, as an advocacy communications team that we're part of, we sit down and see how we can adapt this press release to work in Wales. We can adapt it completely if we feel that will work in Wales – we've got the freedom to do that. But usually, we try to stick to the same messaging because that's the main headline that's going to be coming down the wires ... and then we'll work on adapting the press releases, signing them out for our head of company here, and also sending it to London to be signed off as well ... If it's a huge campaign we need a case study to go with that story ... finding a case study way, way, ahead of the date of the launch ... mainly through our programme work. (Media and communications manager)

Linguistic competency in a bilingual environment was felt to have a significant impact upon the coverage received by campaigns. Some described how working bilingually impacted the levels of expectation and demands placed upon communication professionals in their role:

> The argument's always been is that you just extend your coverage – every time if we've got both the Welsh language media to go to and the English media, and for local radio [we] will tend to do interviews back to back just in both Welsh and English ... it goes out in both languages then. (Media and communications manager)

> It's not an issue, but it's something that could be raised in Wales specifically because it's a bilingual nation. You've got the bilingual media, but you don't necessarily have bilingual experts, so it falls quite often ... onto us, if we happen to be Welsh speakers, to do it and sometimes it really is like, 'I'm only doing it if it's a pre-recorded!' (Media and communications manager)

Others related how, through their experience, they had understood the time and resource pressures faced by journalists and learned what would make their stories more likely to be used:

> Giving them one or two keywords which are, 'that's the story, that's the angle that we can put in that kind of headline', and they can just sort of polish it up and add quotes and they run the story with very little work. So, for stories with the press release, we've found the more work we can do for them, the closer we get to an article they can just upload and

publish, the more likely it will be to get covered – which I can be a criticism of the journalism industry as a whole at the moment, but it is what it is. (Communications officer)

It's a competitive world that we live in and journalists don't have much time, they're on tight deadlines. So, you try and tailor something so it's literally a pick up and plonk job sometimes. (PR and communications manager)

By contrast, several interviewees had no background in media and limited formal training in communications. They reflected upon how this might affect their understanding of what journalists were looking for and the success rate of their press releases:

I would say we probably haven't been as good at it as we possibly could be because we don't have anybody with a media background, you know, so we don't have a PR department or anything like that. It's something that we do sort of tacked onto everything else that we do. (Operational manager)

A lot of them haven't really been picked up … It's a lot more difficult to kind of break into the press really, so it's working out what we need to do for them. Yeah, it's a lot harder because we don't really have the contacts that perhaps we should to find out about how we can do that better. (Information and communications officer)

Interviewees related how trial and error and learning 'on the job' and from 'more senior colleagues' shaped their practice. Whilst media communications training was generally seen as a good thing across the board, for smaller organisations, costs were often identified as an impediment:

I've done the role now for four years or so … I'm doing things my own way which perhaps might not be the best way. There's plenty more training I would like to do and plenty more that is available, but we just simply can't afford [it]. (Information and communications officer)

Training is good, but again, when you work for a third sector organisation, there's not that much money flying around to pay for these things. (Communications officer)

Some interviewees described their responsibility for communications within the remit of much broader roles, with external PR agencies sometimes used to support communications work:

It's just things that we want to focus on and our PR agency helps us with that now. So, every month or two we'll come up with what messages we want to get out there and they'll sort of use their expertise to decide what things are worth doing, then help us with just getting regular stories out, and making sure people know roughly what's going on and things on social media. The PR agency will do bit of that but they also do more targeted pieces. (Knowledge and insight manager)

The communications aims and strategies of those we interviewed varied quite considerably. Whilst some were very clear and focused about their objectives, for others these were less well defined. However, for all of our interviewees, challenging negative public perceptions of those experiencing poverty was seen as a desirable consequence of their work:

It's not about being in people's face. Or being well known or famous, it's the impact of the story on the general public's attitude. (Organisation director)

There are still people out there that have images that food banks feed scruffy lazy so-and-sos and 'if they just got off their butts and got a job', type thing. So, the most effective way to counteract that sort of view and lack of knowledge really, is stories. So when you can tell the story behind the faces … it has much more of an impact, so we're starting to do that. (Operational manager)

However, for some, challenging negative aspects of news agendas and the wider public discourse on poverty was a relatively new, more peripheral or secondary aim. Generating widespread media coverage was less important to their strategies, which instead focused on communicating campaign objectives, reaching policymakers directly and/or highlighting successful activities to funders:

What's important for us is, I guess, what I call a business to business. So we need our funding partners to know that we're doing a good job, which isn't always the same thing as having the wider public know. (Knowledge and insight manager)

The only story we put out was when the First Minister came post-Brexit to reassure migrants that they were still welcome here. But it was driven by the Welsh Government. They wanted to show that people were reassured. From our point of view we weren't concerned about the media angle, we wanted our young people to speak and be heard by the First Minister in a face-to-face situation. From our point of view, the media were just there to tick the box of the Welsh government – to show that the politicians were doing something. So for us, the benefit was just that the children were heard. Not through their media portrayal, although hopefully their media portrayal would have helped create a positive atmosphere. (Organisation director)

We don't have a wider communications strategy in terms of talking to the media or sections of the media. It's something that we're looking at and dipping our toe into the water. Historically it's not something that we've focused on for a number of reasons: team size, the type of work we were doing, lots of reasons really. (Policy and external affairs officer)

Although, for some, communications work was more industry- or funder-oriented, these interviewees also often mentioned how limited and prescribed budgets meant that public communications work was not something which their organisations were able to prioritise or dedicate resources to:

It's not necessarily where we should be spending our charitable money. (Knowledge and insight manager)

Project workers are restricted in what they can do. Everything they do has to be directly towards whatever we've said we were going to do when we got the money, so they're very restricted ... They don't have the time to feedback information to us and we have to go to them to make sure the stories are being shared. (Information and communications officer)

Others expressed concerns that media coverage might not always be helpful to their causes, and that there might be good reason to avoid publicity in some contexts:

We are not looking for a massive story, as huge media attention can always [create] backlashing and negative connotations. So we shy away from massive stories and try to do little stories about volunteering or general contributions on a local level. (Organisation director)

Those who did seek to maximise news coverage for their message often reflected upon the competitive third sector environment and the considerable work entailed in generating a reputation as a good journalistic source for poverty stories:

It's something that is in our longer-term strategy really. To be one of the number one ports of call ... For a small organisation with a small reputation like us, it's getting better. (Policy manager)

When someone is looking around and says, 'alright we need to do this piece of work, who can help us out?' they need to know who we are and what we're about and that we can do that for them. So we need to make sure that's always in people's heads. (Information and communications officer)

I think we've got work to do as well, certainly, with raising our profile with regards to certain issues which we cover, so that we become the 'go to' people. (Media and communications manager)

We need to position ourselves a lot better. I think that when certain stories come out, there's always the expected ... certain organisations are going to react to it because it's to do with them. I don't think, you know, we're the top of the list of anyone. (Information and communications officer)

Many organisations talked about affecting public opinion through news media as just one strategic aim amongst many, others including demonstrating worth to funders, internal or network-partner communications and influencing decision makers:

One is about raising awareness about our organisation – so brand awareness, brand building. The other one is to build awareness for our members and to help raise awareness about the work they do. The third one is to raise awareness within the general public about the issues we talk about – to challenge myths and to show people the reality of what's changed, what's got better, what's got worse. And the fourth one – is challenging key decision-makers and politicians so they can see we need to take action. So, if we go to an Assembly Member that we need to take action so care homes don't go bust, if it's just us saying it, it will be low priority. If we are then saying it's also on BBC Wales, it's more likely to succeed. Sometimes we will do one, which will do all four, and then other times we will just do one. If something is likely to meet those four aims then I would be more likely to put a story out about it and put more time and effort into it. (Policy manager)

I think the responsibility to tell the story of people that we're working with – to demonstrate that homelessness isn't just rough sleeping and also to demonstrate the need of an organisation such as ours in Wales. Whether that's from a point of view of demonstrating our need to the public and getting some engagement in local communities where, you know, we might open a hostel somewhere, and there's some adverse local reaction to that. Obviously, if we can do some proactive positive work before that then we're more accepted into communities. But also from a funding point of view as well – it's all part of the same picture really: just demonstrating our need, demonstrating our outcomes and the continuation of our service then for as long as it needs to be there. (Communications officer)

Another key theme included the work balance to be struck between reacting to media demands and more proactive approaches to communicating story ideas to journalists. Clear differences were evident between how policy-change-oriented organisations, grass-roots service providers and networking/umbrella organisations talked about planning and managing their media strategies:

> We respond to requests from journalists as and when they arrive, and we equally approach them with stories when certain stories come up. So there isn't a formal plan as such. (Organisation director)

> There's an end point, there's a goal that we kind of work back from: so how do we get there, how do we get that reaction or that policy change, or whatever that goal is … and we plan back from that to make sure and assess what the effect of this was and whether we've reached that point. (Media and communications manager)

Many expressed a desire to shift the balance from mainly reactive to more proactive media work in order to position their organisations and/or communicate their message more effectively:

> We can be quite reactive and I think we need to be a bit more proactive. We need to know about things that are going to be happening in advance and have statements prepared. I think a lot of other organisations are good at that, they have contacts in the right places and they know what issues are coming up through the Assembly or local government and they can be prepared for that and have their statement ready, or they can have a quote in the story as it comes out. (Information and communications officer)

> We thought it would be interesting to move from being a very reactive sort of institution where we're literally just there to deal with the fire fighting, and be an institution, which can start, kind of, having a bit of a moral voice, you know, in wider society, and also having a point of view heard in the media about issues like poverty and national social issues. We want to be able to get the messages out there, rather than just being more reactive. (Communications officer)

Whilst some described targeting moments during the calendar year when news media coverage was considered more likely, others described their schedule as directed primarily by campaign priorities and available resources:

> August isn't a bad time because there's a lot less political stories out there so they're a bit more inclined to cover positive stories or particular stories we've had on the backburner that we haven't managed to get out there yet, but send a press release and hope for the best, kind of thing. (Communications officer)

We don't plan around the media news cycle. I know some news organisations do, and try to target when news is tired. But really, our sector moves so quickly that trying to plan ahead for a whole year in terms of media just wouldn't work. So what we tend to do is look for two or three main things we'll focus on that year, put them in the calendar, and then just hope then it gets covered. There are probably organisations who are more easily able to adapt, but we have less resources, which is probably true across the whole sector. (Policy manager)

Whilst mainstream news media channels remained the primary focus of many organisations, social media (primarily Twitter), was also mentioned by almost all interviewees as a channel important for direct campaigning, networking within the sector or with journalists, or managing media communications:

My priority is still very much mainstream media because I think it's still got more power than we have as an organisation to reach people. For example, you get an item on Wales Today: is it 100,000 people watch that? You get something on Good Morning and then of course it goes online. If we can get interviews on Good Morning Wales you're suddenly reaching a lot more people than we can possibly reach through our own communications. (Advisor for communication/media officer)

I think we try and target national rather than regional papers but perhaps for some things we should be targeting regional as well. Personally I don't read newspapers. I'm just of a generation where I don't feel they're as important, but they probably are to other people so it's probably something we need to target a bit more. (Information and communications officer)

I think social media – it's obviously changing the game really when it comes to doing things like grassroots campaigning. And for us, as a larger organisation, [we're] really only just getting to grips with the fact that we can use social media to do things like this to influence. Even on a UK-wide level they're not really doing it much. (Media and communications manager)

More and more there's charities and organisations that are setting up Twitter accounts, especially private Twitter accounts, and inviting journalists to be part of that sort of group. And they send out embargos for press releases via the Twitter account rather than via emails because they get they get lost in emails ... and then, these journalists, they get their part of this exclusive club that gets the information beforehand and you get invited to those accounts. (Media and communications manager)

Despite the importance attributed to public communications by many interviewees, beyond the largest organisations, assessing or accounting for its effectiveness in addressing organisational aims were mostly limited. This was largely attributed to time and resource limitations, although, the use of web and social media analytics was felt to facilitate more monitoring:

> We've got a press monitoring service, Press Data, because they pick up the Welsh language cutting for us and the media unit in London. So we get a news bulletin everyday with a pick up from the press ... London usually picks up online (Wales Online) but the Press Data service we've got here, they will pick up Golwg and Welsh language services as well, so we can monitor our coverage coming in. We usually set up or do the interviews for broadcast, so we know when we've done those; local radio – those get picked up by London as well, and then we record them. So we can look back after a huge campaign and summarise, because London usually wants to know how much gets in the media. (Media and communications manager)

> I haven't got time really to spend too much analysis of how things are being picked up or not. (Advisor for communication/media officer)

> I keep a regular tab on website hits and details of social media weekly and monthly, as well as Facebook, but actually I don't tend to track stories individually, which is perhaps something I should. (Information and communications manager)

> You can see which tweets are most re-tweeted and Twitter analytics shows how many times your page has been viewed. We know it exists, but it's not something we measure. Same with Facebook: the main constraint is time. (Organisation director)

Representation and its challenges

Many third sector interviewees offered views on news media representations of poverty in Wales, as well as their experiences and challenges faced in seeking coverage for their causes. A wide range of issues fed into these broad themes, from reflections upon public opinion and the social/political context for audiences to journalists' specialisms and expertise, the volume and type of coverage, newsworthiness and negative framing.

Overall, many felt that most journalists in Wales were honest and well intentioned in their approach to covering poverty, commenting on differences with UK national media and that a 'tabloid agenda' on poverty was not generally a feature:

> I don't feel like it particularly is in the Welsh media as such. I think they go along with some ... narratives about poverty ... some of which, a

bit negative but … I think less so really local stuff. (Knowledge and insight manager)

My impression is that … they're not they're not too tabloidy … they're not very right wing. They will report it in a fair and accurate way and in a sympathetic way. Advisor for communication/media officer)

I suppose it's not an example from Wales but when you look television programmes like Benefits Street … I'm not sure that's good thing at all. I'm not sure that it … fairly represents those people or those people knew exactly what they were signing up for when they did and that shows people in poverty that is exactly what it shows but … opens them up to all sort of … criticism and scrutiny and I'm … glad Wales hasn't followed suit in that sense. (Communications officer)

I don't think there's' a big difference between Wales and the UK media thinking about it … I think [media organisation] do do that type of story as much as any other tabloid I guess because it's an easy story, you know, 'here's a benefits cheat who was sent to court in wherever' and … you'll get loads of clicks on that you'll get loads of angry comments … because that's what people get angry about very quickly. (Information and communications officer)

Several interviewees reflected upon the particular challenges posed by the Welsh media environment, including a UK–Wales mixed broadcast news and lack of a Wales-based national newspaper, as well as widespread readership of UK national tabloids perceived to negatively influence public opinion on poverty:

Probably the biggest selling newspapers in Wales are not the Western Mail or the Daily Post or the Evening Post it's probably the Sun. So people's opinions of being poor [are influenced] by English based newspapers in Wales. (Advisor for communication/media officer)

It's the red tops … that people are reading – and getting Welsh coverage in them, that's a whole different issue. In Scotland they've got a national media … and people buy into it. We haven't got that in Wales … and I think actually the result of the EU referendum and things like that, there's a whole lot of issues that are connected to that … it's something that we have to deal with and we have to fight against in a way. (Media and communications manager)

So we haven't got either English or Welsh language national paper really covering the whole of Wales … so to get good coverage … in my experience you've got to go for the local weekly papers … it's more difficult but it's one of the most effective ways. It's a lot more hard work than just going to the Guardian and saying can you run this and they'll do it and you know you've got it. (Media and communications manager)

Part of the problem in Wales is we don't have the space to interrogate these issues. We have a Welsh news right, but we still have Newsnight. Sometimes it might be better if we scrapped Newsnight, don't show it on Wales and just focus on our own. We try and do both. If we just had one big one which really explores the issues it might be better. (Policy manager)

There was also appreciation that the news media's coverage of poverty might be affected by the wider public discourse about poverty and/or commercial considerations:

I think journalists would really like to be more honest and be more forceful when talking about poverty but they're coming against the same barriers ... about the sensitivity and the ... political landscape around the issue ... Everybody wants to change a situation it's not right for so many children living in poverty in Wales but it's really difficult to get that honest hard-hitting message out there which also unfortunately is does still not sit comfortably with members of the public. A lot of people turn round and say poverty doesn't exist anymore. (Media and communications manager)

People overestimate the amount of people on benefits the amount of people fraudulently claiming benefits, but I think they perhaps underestimate ... the amount of people in poverty ... If you are on a very low income I'm not sure if people would consider themselves in poverty. (Information and communications officer)

I think that it's about what sells and yeah, there is a human aspect in that and it's also about perpetrating (I was gonna say myth) but perpetrating ideological standpoints of your readership ... you know what they are and you write towards that. (Policy and external affairs officer)

Others felt that the media environment in Wales was also compromised, leading to a less critical approach and inadequate interrogation of the issues, by the proximity of those working in the media and government and NGOs, with a reluctance on the part of third sector organisations to criticise agencies that were ultimately channels for their funding:

The smallness of Wales and the closeness with media and government ... it's quite hard to do really hard hitting journalistic stuff – for the journalists but in particular for the NGOs ... people really cautious to

criticise the government or being seen to criticise government or challenge because their jobs depend on it, or their organisation depends on
funding from them. It's a bit of a strength and a weakness of Wales that
tightness. (Knowledge and insight manager)

As we previously discussed of the journalists' interviews, some third sector interviewees expressed concerns about the diversity of journalism as a profession, and
the extent to which they could represent a diverse population effectively:

I don't think people really, the media really understand poverty properly. A lot of that is who the journalists are: Journalism is a very middle-
class career still … There's not a lot of poorer kids going into journalism.
There seems to be a lot of barriers for journalism becoming representative and diverse body. That can't help in how poverty is represented.
(Organisation director)

I'd like to see more diverse voices involved in the coverage of issues like
poverty. (Communications officer)

I do think in Wales there's a big emphasis on bilingualism, which is
good, I do support it, but I do think that adds more barriers to diversity
in terms of class and ethnicity. So more middle-class white people are
more likely to speak Welsh than a working-class Muslim, or black person. But that's just statistically the case. A lot of Cardiff-based journalists
in particular are from a particular section of society which isn't necessarily a good cross section. (Organisation director)

A theme commonly commented on was the attention afforded to poverty in
the Welsh media, with interviewees differing in their views of how accurate
current portrayals are, and how they felt they should be. Some highlighted the
prevalence of experiences of poverty, pointing to employment insecurity and
the diversity of people facing economic hardship. Others pointed to the ten-
dency to overgeneralise about poverty in Wales:

It seems to be a lot more in the news … I'm not sure if that's just
because I pay attention to it more because I work in it or it is actually
improving. It seems to me … well it's a lot bigger an issue, especially
… since the recession obviously it's been a lot more of a common issue
to talk about … child poverty, fuel poverty, lots of different kinds of
poverty, older people as well has been a big deal. (Information and
communications officer)

I think what would be great is if they could highlight … we've got real
problems with poverty in Wales and … it's getting worse rather than

better. If you'd said ten years ago there'd be all these food banks around and all our time would be taken up ... with just trying to put enough food for people to eat you would never have thought it would have happened in this country. (Advisor for communication/media officer)

It has had quite a lot of attention, but I don't think the links are made very effectively. I think sometimes the media characterises the whole of Wales as poor, the poor relation, that poverty is a problem throughout Wales ... You know plenty of people in Wales are really well off. (Organisation director)

I've worked in social care of one sort or another for more years than I care to remember and I think that I think the face of poverty has changed considerably in that time ... there was very much 'them and us' ... and now the people that are using services are a much broader demographic than they were back then ... and I think the media need to make sure they reflect that. (Operational manager)

I think certainly in Wales that the stories that I've seen ... they have been broader and whether that's to do with the stories we are feeding the media and maybe we're getting better at getting that message out ... or whether that is because the media are actually recognising it and choosing to reflect that I don't know ... you know it could be anybody it could be you, could be your neighbour, could be anybody you know and to actually get that across to people ... the more we can do that the more effective we can be. (Operational manager)

I think a lot of sort of hidden poverty ... basically a family can be ... both parents can be employed working a full time ... low paying wage but full time ... and they can ... from outward signs have home have stability but actually they don't have enough to cover their ... basic expenses and it's ... a daily struggle, they just get by and that kind of poverty I think is very much under the radar and I think it's becoming more and more common ... Really being on the cusp of things is really difficult so I think sometimes poverty is represented from the extreme examples of ... absolutely being destitute ... you might be 'there' one day, but you are really just a few bad payments and bills away from being right at the other end and it's a sort of stressful existence and I think understanding the sort of instability and stress of it associated with poverty I think doesn't always get come across. (Communications officer)

Many interviewees felt that there was a lack of context provided in much poverty-related coverage, with insufficient examination of the causes of the difficulties people might find themselves and associated social issues:

It's almost like taboo isn't it? … When the media report homelessness … especially in the filming aspect, it tends to be in one way so – it is … 'oh look at this person on the street!' and then it always is that person, the sad person with a dog … and then it doesn't really delve deeper into maybe why that person is like that and how easy it could be for … you or I to be [in that situation]. (PR and communications manager)

When Islamophobia is spoken about in the media you know it's … the street thug calling someone you know a Paki on the street and not the sort of wider social issues which is much more damaging and much more crippling to society. So, I think that's also maybe something that needs to be looked at when we talk about what poverty is … it can't be separated out from all the other types of discrimination people are facing. (Communications officer)

Whilst third sector organisations' perceptions of what may be newsworthy were not dissimilar to those of the journalists we interviewed, many related how certain topics or projects they had tried to communicate had been ignored, or regretted that stories that they would like to see appearing in the media were unlikely to be covered. Whilst some of these differences were clearly determined by their particular campaign messages and/or the target audiences they were trying to reach, other more general issues were also cited. In general, as some journalists acknowledged, the unattractiveness of poverty as a topic and the notion that people may be averse to hearing about it was raised:

We [talk about] poverty but of course poverty … isn't sexy and I think if when you look at poverty you also look at how do they report wealth – and that gets a lot of reporting, doesn't it, through celebrities, through … high powered things … that's what attracts people, that's what people want to read about. Maybe it comes back down to, we don't want to read bad news about [sad people]. (Advisor for communication/media officer)

Conversely, however, many also reflected upon how 'good news' tended to be ignored or seen as less newsworthy:

Sometimes it just feels like positive news isn't wanted – it's … 'aw, we want doom and gloom and we want to report that side', like the sadder side of things because that's what people want to read and it's … quite sad really, and you know your positive news story could get bumped. (PR and communications manager)

It's a lot harder to sell a story of something good that happens because … the good things happening … should be the default for things. (Information and communications officer)

> Good news doesn't sell and I think that's a great shame ... I think there
> is a realisation ... an awareness that people don't want to read negative
> news all the time ... that'll hopefully benefit us. (Advisor for communi-
> cation/media officer)

Reflections upon other difficulties with news values focused on sensationalism
and the idea that interesting but not extraordinary stories tended to be ignored,
with the result that the reality of poverty is not accurately portrayed. Amongst
other examples which resonated with journalists' accounts, this included the
idea that the nature of poverty as an ongoing issue is generally not represented:

> With uniqueness, the media always say that Wales is experiencing
> high levels of poverty and that nothing has changed. Is it a big thing
> if Wales is always being talked about and poverty? So things that tend
> to get news coverage are big changes, new initiatives that are unique.
> (Policy manager)

> UK-wide there was an increase in children living in poverty accord-
> ing to the stats, but in Wales there was a 2% decrease from last year.
> So we reacted to it anyway, because it was still two-thirds – almost two-
> thirds of children in Wales living in poverty ... because it wasn't sort of
> an increase I think some papers ... picked up on the UK story instead
> because it was more of a big deal I guess, but they didn't pick up on the
> Welsh angle. (Media and communications manager)

> A lot of the time the people that we support ... are still on a journey,
> they're nowhere near finished, but I would argue that that is not interest-
> ing to a journalist. They want the person that's had 'bad-better-good' ...
> it's that formula ... I think it's a bit redundant really sometimes ... not
> everyone is cookie cutter like that especially not the people that we work
> with. (PR and communications manager)

For some, the important stories they felt were ignored were those with more
specialised or technical aspects, for example with regard to housing policy and
its consequences and connections to wider economic currents:

> You will sometimes get the narrative that it brings in jobs and will help
> support the ... local micro economies ... and I think as a sector we con-
> tinue to pursue that narrative. So most house building for the social
> sector will have a community benefits package which is an agreement
> ... with the house builders ... about employing a certain number of
> individuals ... from the local community or offering apprenticeships
> or training schemes. So there's something that's actually tangible that's
> going back into that community but we don't hear about that in the

media ever and that's quite interesting … housing isn't … massively in the media I would say. (Policy and external affairs officer)

In areas of social housing, such as supported housing, which is a housing project which supports people with additional needs. Currently no cap applies to them. Westminster suggest capping that rate, I know that is quite technical but what it means is that suddenly those organisations, would not be able to get additional money from local authorities, so all that supported accommodation would go. So the impact would be catastrophic. But it's not anywhere in the media. It would have a huge impact on poverty in Wales. It's starting to be talked about a bit, but the problem is it's a little too complicated to explain. So anything that takes longer than ten seconds to explain it won't get covered. (Policy manager)

Other influences upon a story's newsworthiness and what 'gets it out there' resonated strongly with the reflections of journalists. These included proximity – especially in terms of demonstrating the specific relevance of a wider, UK story for Wales:

Stories have to be Welshified. (Advisor for communication/media officer)

Because we're working with London and the other devolved nations as well, it's quite a big impact especially if it's a UK-wide story … so our work here is trying to get a Welsh angle to a UK-wide story and make it work … for the media here so that's our challenge. (Media and communications manager)

For similar reasons, it was felt that stories about charity overseas and/or foreign aid tended to be ignored by the Welsh media, unless some kind of Welsh angle could be included. The combination of certain elements, such as strong statistics backed up with a sense of urgency or emotion surrounding a poverty issue, was identified to enhance the newsworthiness of stories:

A good stat usually grabs the headlines and then you just pad out that stat then with your case study or maybe a story – depends what else is going on … normally there needs to be some kind of emotional response to the issue to make it successful … and if possible some sort of urgency as well … you need something that people are going to feel emotive about for the journalists to pick up on it as well to make it a big story I think. (Media and communications manager)

However, for others, sometimes the reasons for a story being either picked up or ignored were difficult to identify and could appear rather arbitrary:

It's really hard to know which ones are going to work when you do. So there's one that didn't which was really surprising, because ... I thought everything in there was a powerful story and that general readers would care about and it didn't get picked up ... Maybe something else was going on that day, maybe we didn't make it clear enough ... Sometimes when you're not expecting it you suddenly have a big push out of nowhere, then other times you generate interest and end up getting nothing. (Policy manager)

We can't force ... it's up to them to follow their agenda and of course it's up to the will of the particular producer ... particular editors at the time what stories they're going ... to do and of course we know we're competing against every other. A lot of it is so arbitrary – that's what we're dealing with. There aren't hard and fast rules ... and you know you can write the best possible press release and one day it'll get in and it'll get front page it'll be on Wales Today and another day it'll be completely ignored it all depends on what else is [in]. (Advisor for communication/ media officer)

Some, however, discussed how legal restrictions such as purdah in the run-up to elections, or a more general concern that taking an overtly political stance on the issues of the day would not be helpful, restricted the kinds of coverage third sector organisations themselves sought to pursue. For example, with regard to the EU referendum and Brexit:

We didn't really say anything about it after reading through charity commission/electoral commission rules – we thought it was easier to just stay out of it. However as soon as the referendum was decided, the next day, we put out a very strong statement – not condemning the result, but saying we were disappointed with the result and then following that, about how the fallout of the results ... will continue to affect people. We've come out very strongly against it afterwards but we didn't say anything in the run up because ... as a publicly funded charity we can't be seen to influence people's votes ... some of those things ... are a little tricky sometimes ... when there are really big issues we feel we should be commenting on, but we just kind of can't, we have to hold back a little bit. (Information and communications officer)

Because we receive government funding I don't think we would've said a word really about it and I think if there is ever a time to talk about poverty it should've been during Brexit. So I'm gutted on a personal level ... I think the remain campaign did a terrible job in Wales ... if there was ever a time to look at areas that are socially deprived and look at what European money has brought in it was then ... then I think we could have done with hard hitting in your face kind of stories, but [it] just didn't come and it's sort of afterwards now people are like, 'aw, aw yeah we do get EU money so it's just a nightmare'. (PR and communications manager)

Finally, in terms of representation, whilst most accepted that different perspectives on poverty should be featured in the news, many talked about the power of negative media framing as something that was exploited and damaging, often pointing to problematic documentaries and news coverage in the UK media. Others also objected specifically to things they had observed when journalists in Wales 'framed' a story, such as posing loaded questions, or reproducing myths about the 'deserving' and 'undeserving' poor:

> Every message we get is filtered through questions that they ask and how they frame those expressions … Asking a question about what to do about homeless people on drugs: that kind of framing, for every person who is listening, they now have the idea that people are homeless because of drugs. So whatever we say then becomes negative. What would be good is if they asked neutral questions. If we are trying to be evasive then be as intrusive as you like, but if the news story is positive, like a new initiative to help rough sleepers, we don't need that almost antagonistic question … if they continue to frame it in that way, people's empathy for people in poverty will be damaged. (Policy manager)

> So the interviewer would say, 'So what about people who say that some homeless people don't deserve help?' And maybe it's a trick way of asking the question. The whole question accepts the premise that there are people who aren't worthy of help. And that trickles through in a lot of articles, that there is the deserving poor and the undeserving poor … I'd rather say on the radio interview, 'no every poor person deserves help', but you don't want to derail the interview so instead you say, 'no, that's not the majority of people, most homeless people are just falling on hard times.' So I think it's the way the media frames the questions, which pushes you down a certain path which is difficult to correct. (Policy manager)

> what's interesting around disability is the narrative around that falls into two camps you've got the deserving disabled poor people, 'aren't they poor!' and it's very disempowering, and then you've got, 'oh well, you're not disabled enough so you shouldn't be getting the money and you're scrounging!' (Policy and external affairs officer)

> The topic is hard. We can use facts to counter the myths of homelessness, we can say, 'no, it's not true, it's relationship breakdown', or 'not all

homeless people are ex-offenders'. I think when you talk about benefits, people have a block to any facts – so the fact that most benefits are pensions, yet we spend all our time talking about disability, unemployment allowance. That really bothers me. (Policy manager)

Whilst the consequences for public opinion and empathy were clearly identified as at stake in these reflections, more immediate negative and direct impacts of negative media (and political) discourses on poverty upon those who needed to seek support from the third sector were also discussed:

To get people to come forward to help with benefits … when they're being shown on the media as, 'they're all scroungers', actually when politicians themselves are saying, 'they're scroungers, all you have to do is work hard and you'll be fine' you know there are people that can't do that and when the rate of benefit fraud is 0.1% but the public perception of it was … into like double figures … but then people genuinely need … to come to us to help to apply for those benefits because your chances of doing it alone are quite small. The chances of doing it with us are very high … I think generally people shouldn't be ashamed of applying for benefits but that's … the impression they get, I think, from the mainstream media. (Information and communications officer)

Relationships with the media

Interviewees reflected extensively upon how reacting and responding to media demands formed part of their work. Engaging with journalists' requests were usually motivated by the sense that negative ideas about poverty might be challenged through promoting more representative, accurate stories about people and/or positive outcomes of their work. However, a concern that campaign priorities and organisational values should not be compromised was very evident and the difficulties of managing responses to journalists alongside casework were also a strong theme in these accounts. Many, for example, talked about the time pressures for journalists, but also in their own organisations' front-line work, and how this impacted upon finding case studies:

If there are … big news stories, like when we send out our annual statistics for instance, we very often will be the point of contact for Wales, so I get quite a lot of phone calls from journalists who want a story, preferably with a client, within the next half an hour please! So there's always the time pressure, which I understand, and there's always the demand for a client, because obviously, if you've got a person you know it makes the story more sellable I suppose. (Operational manager)

Getting those stories from the project workers is not always straight-forward, simply because of their caseload … They have a great solution for one of their clients -they're kind of signed off: 'great, move on to the next one'. They've got another twenty! But, they haven't got time to feedback that story then – to get that out. (Information and communications officer)

Sometimes they're looking for someone and the timeframe's just completely unworkable. For a start, I might not be able to respond for an issue for a few hours and then you've got to do the digging. So, if they're looking for someone and then trying to convince that person … I mean we don't have a full time media person, so that tends to be something very, very, difficult because everyone's doing a working day … Even the people they want to interview or speak to might have a working day … Sometimes we need at least a few days just to get things going and yeah, we've missed a few boats because we just can't respond to the pace at which they're working. (Communications officer)

Others emphasised the difficulty in accommodating very specific requests from journalists, especially at short notice and with limited resources:

Sometimes it's very specific what they're looking for as well, and you're just like, that's too narrow a field, you know, that's ridiculous! (PR and communications manager)

'Have you got a case study for this afternoon? I'm interviewing the Children's Commissioner on poverty, and I know you're working on poverty. Have you got a family [laughing] available this afternoon around six?' 'Well, of course, no!' (Media and communications manager)

If, say, a broadcast journalist gives us a ring and says, 'we've got this story going out tomorrow, have you got someone we can come and interview? We need to be there in two hours and we need them to tell us their life story', that's really hard, and sometimes in Welsh as well, which is always a 'no' because, do you know, it's the holy trinity of finding someone who's available, happy to talk about their story, and then in Welsh, or in the area. (Communications officer)

Various strategies for anticipating, managing and responding to such demands were suggested by interviewees, from simply declining and/or suggesting others that might be able to respond, preparing materials that could be shared online for journalists to access, and proactively preparing 'banks' of case studies as part of their project work:

We do get maybe a couple a month asking, but, as I say, it's usually fairly short notice, fairly specific, and there's not something we can directly help out with. But then, I'll be happy to pass them onto organisations that I know may be able to help. (Information and communications officer)

I think one of the things we learnt is if a journalist comes to us and it's … really really really tight, just say no from the beginning. Because, one thing is we might, try and then everyone goes away unhappy because we put in the effort and we haven't found anyone and they feel like we've let them down … I think that's just a lot fairer than … saying there might be someone, 'let me see' and then come back at the end of those 24 hours and say, 'no, there isn't.' (Communications officer)

Every month or so, what the media department – there's all of two of them (laughs) – say is basically, 'please keep clients' stories in your heads as something that we constantly want'. So, they use those for all sorts of things, and we're starting to do it on our website: so we're using client feedback and stories to put on our website to make it more meaningful, to make it more real. So, the idea is, then, they've got a bank of stories they can pull on and they're not then running round trying to find somebody – that's the theory. (Operational manager)

What we're trying to do is build up a bank of people that are willing to talk to the media, so when we do get those calls, we just give them a call saying, 'do you mind doing an interview for BBC this afternoon?' (Media and communications manager)

Case studies (people willing to share their stories publicly) were widely identified as one of the most important elements that would make a story, proactively offered to the media, more likely to be picked up by journalists. However, some interviewees were keen to explain how generating media interest in case studies was just one step in a process requiring careful management:

If we have a campaign coming up, we've got our case study in place, it's then two days before: I'm just phoning around sending the press release out under embargo and making it quite clear we have got a case study to go with this story. Boom! The phone's dashing straight away because it's a package … Sending the story out, if we can, two days, three days before, to give enough time for broadcasters to go out and interview the case studies – especially if it's a weekend story ready for Monday morning – it's in the bag then. And you've tried to give that family enough time as well, because ITV, BBC, Western Mail, radio stations will all want to talk to that case study … They're the human interest story, they're the important people. We can fit the spokespeople in here around any time flexible enough, but the human interest story, that's going to bring the story alive isn't it? So, trying to tie in enough time so they don't get overwhelmed ... I've been in a situation where BBC's gone in, I've got ITV on the doorstep ready to come in, and a queue of journalists ready to go in to the family inside, and it was a matter of just keeping them ... like a queuing system. We try not to get to that situation – try to do maybe one in the morning, one in the afternoon, and the others [later]. (Media and communications manager)

Managing journalists' approaches in order to protect clients from potentially negative aspects of media attention was highlighted in various accounts. Interviewees were intensely aware of their ethical responsibilities and duty of care towards the vulnerable people they represented or supported in their work. They were also very aware of the risks that a story handled badly could pose to the reputation of their organisations or even the wider sector. These concerns underpinned a strong rationale for maintaining close contact with case study participants, preparing them for the experience and supervising the interactions they had facilitated with journalists. These precautions for protecting people who had agreed to relate their experiences of poverty were balanced against what interviewees perceived was the potential value of this work:

Our media work tends to be about getting people in touch with the right case studies. It's not that important to us that they know who [we are], but that they know that homelessness in Wales is working, that they get case studies and that the message is getting out. Sometimes the wrong case study is put forward, or the wrong message is put out. So we always try to make sure that when they go on the radio or news, they say the right thing and protecting what the sector is trying to stand for. (Policy manager)

We can't just pluck them out of their lives in an hour or so and give out numbers and say, 'yeah, just ring this person, ask them about what it's like to live in poverty'. It's of course a sensitive issue, isn't it, and you're working with families that don't necessarily know that they're living in poverty. How do you approach that? (Media and communications manager)

I think we are fairly cautious when it comes to the way that we deal with filming in particular. The longer I'm here the more I understand that because the people that we're dealing with do have different issues and are vulnerable and we do have a duty of care – it's ethical it's moral – and, you know, I wouldn't want to be the organisation that is putting our people on the TV for the sake of having exposure, I just don't think it's worth it. (PR and communications manager)

> They seem to take one element and want to expose that and you're like, 'well, that's not a true reflection, and why would we give you access to our staff and our service users for you to do that?' We've got a duty of care as well because we get funding from Welsh government and you can imagine … We have a good relationship with them and we don't want to blur those lines either, so there's lots at stake when we think about what we are willing to put out there. (PR and communications manager)

Interviewees acknowledged it could be difficult to find people willing to share their stories for public consumption, even if those stories could potentially illuminate important broader issues:

> People who are accessing the services don't necessarily want that to be public. They don't want everyone to know that they're claiming Personal Independence Payments because they can't work, or seeking support for their mental health. So that's difficult sometimes – to get personalised case studies – they're kind of quite sensitive areas unfortunately. It would be great to get some of those stories out there but because they are sensitive, it's difficult to do so. (Information and communications officer)

Contrastingly, others related how people were, perhaps quite surprisingly, often willing to share their stories and prepared to put themselves forward as case studies for journalists:

> A lot of our volunteers and certainly a lot of colleagues (and myself previously) are always a bit reticent to ask clients if they'll tell their stories. There's always an assumption that people won't want to say – that they're embarrassed, they won't want to tell anybody. But actually, my experience has been that when you ask, I'd say almost (let's be conservative) 85% of people said, 'yeah, no problem'. Some people would have a proviso that they do it anonymously, which is fair enough. I think there are a lot more people who are actually quite happy to share their story and whether that's a change in attitude, I don't know. I wonder if the views of people who are poor have shifted slightly because there are so many more of them … because of austerity and the years of financial, you know, where there are more and more and more people who are working, who are doing all the things you're supposed to do and yet still struggling, or still find themselves in crisis, and actually, has that reduced stigma a bit? (Operational manager)

Yet, many warned that case study participants were not always necessarily fully cognisant of the potential consequences of sharing their stories, even when organisations took care to explain honestly what their participation would involve:

> I remember working on one story and it was [an] action group in the Valleys. I got some lovely case studies from people who've been helped hugely by this organisation and I explained to them, 'you know it's for the media, happy to talk?', 'yes, yes very happy!' Did the interviews, then they saw it in print and had a breakdown. And you feel [sighs], I think you have to recognise that they're vulnerable people and they will say, 'yes, yes', perhaps not really completely understanding that they're going to open the paper and see themselves in there, and they're going to feel unhappy about that, and they're not very stable. So, you've got to be really careful with that. (Advisor for communication/media officer)

> He had some photographs taken. Then, a few days later they sent a photographer down. The thing this illustrates, that we obviously have a responsibility to people that we're working with to protect them a little bit and to point out that anything they put out there is going to be there forever. You know, if he's going for a job in five years time and they Google his name, this might come up. So, we have to be very responsible to the people, the stories that we're telling. I guess journalists don't have the same level of responsibility towards people, hence the slightly insensitive headline. (Communications officer)

Especially for those working directly with clients, whilst the argument for publicising people's stories was understood, many felt that taking part in case studies often simply did not serve the interests of the individuals involved. This was due to participants' vulnerability to the risks of exposure, including feelings of intrusion during the interview itself, the consequences experienced in the immediate aftermath of publicity or its future ramifications in their lives. As such, some interviewees explained their great reluctance to put anybody forward as case studies:

> Well there's this thing called poverty porn. Where poor people are used by the media, sometimes, to get the sob story element and so we usually don't, when people ask for refugee, or asylum seeker or child refugee. We'll ask our clients, because we are the middleman, we don't want to prevent anyone from taking up that opportunity. But generally we don't see it as a benefit for the individual as it can do more harm than good. But sometimes I can see the argument for why a really good example of a family or individual who is in a situation of poverty, how that can inspire people to feel more empathy, and give more money towards refuges and people on benefits. Whatever it is. I can see the arguments for having those stories in the media. But more often than not I don't

think it benefits the individual. Maybe the cause but not the individuals. (Organisation director)

We are getting more and more requests people wanting to speak to Syrian refugees, so actually to the beneficiaries of our services. In this case we would usually ask our clients first, so a refugee client or a family, in a sensitive way. Most of the times it's not something we end up doing because the families don't really want to do it. We can't see it's going to benefit them. It's probably going to expose them to more harm than good. Usually we avoid bringing individual clients into the media spotlight just because of potential ramifications we can't control once the story has gone out. So usually we would just give a generic comment without identifying individuals. So it's quite difficult to manage properly, even though with the promises of anonymity, there's still an element of risk. (Organisation director)

Their families are concerned they might be a target for people from the Far Right, and if you think of the Jo Cox situation, it isn't an impossibility. There's always these potential problems, where young people could become a target, or anyone who speaks out on these issues. (Organisation director)

Others described the practical steps they took to try to protect vulnerable people who did decide to cooperate with the media on stories. These included concealing identities, profiling an organisation's work from a distance, putting up spokespeople instead of clients or releasing agreed statements:

The people who were eating there because they were hungry or didn't have homes, didn't have food, we just made sure that they didn't get any cameras near them. Some of them were asylum seekers who had showed their case. We just didn't want to expose them at all to any sort of scrutiny, so we just made sure that they knew that these guys were here and they could just keep their distance and there's hundreds of people there so it's fine. (Communications officer)

A lot of the stories we've collected we probably couldn't put out there because of the vulnerability of the person ... and then it's like, well, do you put an anonymised version? Would that even be picked up? I'm not sure, it's a difficult one. (PR and communications manager)

It may be better to speak to someone who's in charge of whatever the situation is that person is in. So for example, if it's a story about a hostel, rather than talk to somebody who's using the hostel, talk to the hostel manager who will have a much broader experience and be able to talk to you on a more informed, broader basis, and who probably would be happy to have a photograph taken and to have the story recorded. (Advisor for communication/media officer)

As soon as anything happens to put them in the media spotlight they [affiliate organisations] do instinctively come to us and we're happy with that and we try and speak to them about it. I think it's generally because a lot of them again wouldn't have those skills, so they're hoping we can give them a bit of a hand with it. There was a case where the [affiliate organisation] wasn't giving any statements at all, and they just said go straight to the [umbrella organisation] and we had a prepared press release on it. They know that basically what's going out there is going to be coherent. (Communications officer)

Others described the work they did to prepare and support people through meetings with journalists and the subsequent coverage, and to follow up afterwards in providing further support:

I just give them a really honest overview of what it'll mean: There'll be journalists wanting to speak to you over the phone and wanting to come to your house; there'll be cameras in the house; there'll be articles about you in the paper; you'll be asked to have your picture taken. And also, the other thing that's become apparent over the years – the online aspects of it – of course they go on, as well, to see all these comments coming up, so you've got to really prepare them for those (mostly positive) comments. But there could be one or two negative ones, and those are the ones that are going to hurt. (Media and communications manager)

The journalists know I'm there with them during that interview – journalist rings my mobile phone and I'll just put it on to whoever's doing the interview. So, I'm there at all times. If they're doing an interview with television and involved with print journalists as well, if they want a neutral area, we can invite them over here and do it here. Because a lot of people are not happy having cameras and journalists going into their home. (Media and communications manager)

We try then to keep in touch with a case study: not sort of zooming in, taking over their lives for a couple of days and then, 'bye, thank you!' You know, we try to keep that relationship warm. I'll try and go back to see them the day after, 'how are you? What kind of response have we had to the story? Who's seen you on telly? Anything on social media you're not happy with?' Just to give that support – it's a really tough process – then you're not just leaving them with it themselves only. (Media and communications manager)

Many interviewees reflected upon the extent to which journalists appreciated these sensitivities and the role of communications professionals in facilitating and mediating contact with case studies. Some described cooperative relationships with journalists very positively, and appreciated how some journalists listened to third sector expertise about managing people's vulnerabilities, set against the pressures they faced in producing stories:

> They've got a story as well, and they've got maybe an editor or a producer that wants specific things from them, and sometimes it's trying to meet in the middle. It's kind of like, 'well, if you want that, we can give you that but we can't give you THAT', and it's almost trying to work together and I think some journalists are more aware of that than others. (PR and communications manager)

> It actually quite refreshing when we are talking to [broadcaster] that they are aware of the sensitivities around homelessness and we've said, you know, 'if you want to cover a story with us then we do have things that we do need you to comply with' and they seem very happy to do so, which is really nice. The independent production companies that have come and met with us haven't been as, sort of, forthcoming: it's like, 'we've got this story, we've got this idea, we're putting it out there, it's gonna be, like, gritty' and you're like, 'it seems that you will go to any length to sort of get what you want to portray on screen, and that's really not where we're coming from.' (PR and communications manager)

Others talked about more difficult experiences with journalists, with tensions arising due to the manner of their approach, issues of control and the value of a story set against its potential harms:

> But I did find them quite aggressive in how much pressure they put on us. When we were able to do it, we had the [third sector organisation], but their board didn't want to subject their young people to that scrutiny, so their board didn't want to agree with it. So we informed [broadcaster] then the journalist was very aggressive, and they independently bi-cut us and went directly to the [third sector organisation] then offered them all these reassurances. In the end they did agree, but because I said no and they went against me, I felt they were quite aggressive and persistent. They just wanted their three minutes of racist kids on TV. But they weren't. So they weren't that nice to deal with. (Organisation director)

> Journalists are very ethical, responsible people, but it has happened to me over the years that the families have been contacted directly. And then you've got no control then of how what they are saying is going to be interpreted in the press. They don't know how to handle press

because you can't give them that level of support then ... Especially as they're doing it for your organisation we try to support them as much as you can, especially if they're young people as well. (Media and communications manager)

I think that they have to understand that you can't always get a case – you can't: it's unreasonable to get case studies from people who are who are vulnerable. (Advisor for communication/media officer)

Some of these tensions were eased in situations where third sector interviewees felt they had trusted contacts in the media. Many talked about developing a trusted media contact list, often through events and networking, as a desirable and important aspect of their practice, and something that would contribute to their message being represented well in the news:

We've developed a relationship with individual journalists. Which is how our stories get in the paper. We don't have that relationship with other newspapers. So we will prepare a press release, send it out, then sometimes journalists will get back to us and say this is how we're going to frame the story. More often, they don't actually have the time to come back to us, we give them the press release, we trust them anyway to know that they're going to present the story positively. And then the story goes out. (Organisation director)

It's good to build a relationship outside of a news context, outside of the news cycle, to kind of get to know someone. And that's very useful, as well, for when you actually want to get a story out because you can approach them and say, 'Ah we want to get this story out there, what's the best way of doing it?' He might give some advice then about how we can pitch it and angle it, and so those relationships are actually quite important and useful to us. (Communications officer)

There are certain journalists in Wales that I have actually used specifically for certain stories ... I would give them an exclusive first. So for example, we've got a report coming out in four weeks, so a [journalist] is coming in for a meeting to have a look at the report even before we write a press release to see whether they will run a whole scoop sort of thing. So, I would say relationships like that in Wales are easy to develop. (Public affairs officer)

Others felt that either they knew too few journalists well enough or had not secured the kinds of working relationships with the media that would support their communications practices and saw this very much as something in which they should invest time and effort:

I think we're doing quite well in the South, but like I'd like us to be able to have journalists throughout Wales that we know are susceptible to us putting stuff out and us getting coverage, and I think that is achievable. It's just you've got to put some work in, pick up the phone and, if you can, go and meet them. Someone will have a coffee with you if you ask. It's sort of reciprocal as well, so them coming to us for comments, especially in North Wales, I would like them to identify us as a big charity up there. (PR and communications manager)

I think it's fair to say we've not got strongly developed relationships with journalists. I think that's something that we'd like to improve. We are building on it because it's a case of once you get a good relationship with a person you do tend to go back to them. (PR and communications manager)

However, all of our interviewees mainly focused on their relationships with the media in Wales, with some expressing significant aversion to media such as the national tabloids thought to pursue a negative approach towards those experiencing poverty:

I would never dream of e-mailing a tabloid newspaper, never, because I don't trust them. From what I can see, they have an agenda, which is diametrically opposed to our own. They seem to be more about highlighting and creating divisions, when we are not about that. (Organisation director)

Finally, many interviewees reflected upon the things they believed could make a positive difference to their practice and to the coverage of poverty in the media in Wales. Here, the issue of cooperation, both with other charities or NGOs and also with the media, was regularly mentioned in different ways. Some of this revolved around preparing for media requests and proactively working on time-sensitive materials such as case studies in advance. People talked about working together to combine their skills and work specialisms – especially with regard to connecting small or service-delivery-focused organisations working directly with clients with those with more resources and expertise dedicated to communications, who worked daily with the media. Several interviewees suggested building 'story banks' or maintaining up-to-date records of those willing to offer their stories as case studies in one way or another. Coming together to share these resources, to work towards collective strategic goals or projects, was proposed, as was seeking more opportunities to learn from journalists what their priorities were for stories about poverty. Interviewees were evidently keen that initiatives be taken that encouraged mutual understanding of the respective roles played by diverse third sector organisations working on poverty and by journalists in the production of poverty news.

Third sector experiences: a summary

Third sector professionals were broadly positive overall in their views and experiences of the news media in Wales. With some exceptions, the majority were keen to form strong working relationships with news media in order to communicate stories about their work and to highlight the various ways in which poverty is an issue. However, there was a considerable variance in the degree to which interviewees expressed confidence about their existing relationships with media and the capacity and resources available within their organisations for cultivating them. Often those working for larger policy- or advocacy-focused organisations had valuable experience to draw on, from working either in the media and/or in communications-dedicated roles. With clear strategies, time, resources and expertise dedicated to media communications, both responding to journalists' requests for help and proactively placing stories were clearly seen as far more feasible than for smaller, grass-roots organisations. For smaller and more front-line service-delivery-focused organisations, time and resource constraints often meant that media communications really did not factor as a strategic priority, even if interactions with journalists did happen to varying degrees as part of their work. However, at the grass roots, interviewees were clearly much more directly connected to valuable first-hand accounts of people experiencing poverty than those in larger organisations, where such case studies had to be 'found'.

Most third sector interviewees recognised the value of case studies to newsmakers, and as a means through which to represent the realities of poverty compellingly and meaningfully. However, without exception, third sector interviewees also voiced concern about the potential harms facing case study participants and the duty of care upon them to protect those to whom they facilitated media access. Several talked with experience about the need to prepare people for, manage and follow up on their encounter with the media in order to fulfil this duty. A clear tension was evident between, on the one hand, the potential value attributed to case studies in achieving communications goals and affecting the wider discourse on poverty and whether, on the other, interviewees believed case studies served the interests of individuals participating.

Across the range of organisations, interview participants clearly shared many goals and key values, focusing upon supporting those in need, improving lives and seeking to transform the conditions underlying experiences of poverty. However, communication aims were also driven by other considerations, such as generating organisational funding and recognition. Indeed, an important theme underpinning many of the reflections of our interviews with third sector professionals was the competitive environment in which they work. Yet, overall, the interviews highlighted a willingness in the sector to cooperate on communicating a fair and accurate narrative on poverty in Wales.

Summary of key findings

- Welsh media coverage of poverty was thematically focused on news about the economy and/or politics, and during our monitoring period (April–July 2016) was driven by Welsh Government policy/politics, business news and the EU referendum campaign.
- Only a third of coverage featuring poverty focused on it as the main story – more often poverty appears as an incidental, contextualising or background subject in reports on politics or discussions of macroeconomic policy.
- Connections were seldom explicitly made between nationally significant stories about politics or the economy and their possible impacts on livelihoods and experiences of poverty in Wales at the personal or community level.
- The main issues associated with poverty were unemployment and job insecurity. Social deprivation more generally also featured large in poverty narratives across media.
- There was no significant evidence of blaming the vulnerable and those suffering hardship for their experiences of poverty, economic inequality or social disadvantage.
- People affected by poverty were more likely to be identified in broad terms (as communities or the public in general) than specific demographic groups. Workers were a key focus, however, located in a variety of areas of Wales.
- The possible causes and consequences of poverty were often left unmentioned in the coverage. As such, reporting did not offer a contextualising framework for understanding the why poverty arises and why it matters as an issue.
- Where contextualising details were included, structural factors, including the legacy for the Welsh economy of deindustrialisation, were framed as the primary contextualising cause of poverty issues. The general sense that communities suffer was the most frequently mentioned consequence of poverty.
- On Brexit, voting to leave the European Union was more likely to be positioned as responsible for poverty, compromising future prosperity and livelihoods than voting to remain/remaining in the EU. However, coverage connecting either Brexit or remaining in the EU to poverty issues was not prevalent until well into the referendum campaign.

- Government, and in particular the Welsh Government, was most likely to be positioned as responsible for poverty-related issues and to be responding or expected to respond to it. However, the UK national government and business also featured significantly as responsible parties.
- Political voices were the most regularly cited sources in the coverage of poverty, although business sources and citizens' perspectives also featured strongly. Overall, more than twice as many male sources were cited than female.
- A relationship of co-dependence already exists between journalists and the third sector in reporting poverty. Third sector professionals recognised mainstream news as crucial for communicating ideas that condition public attitudes on poverty. Journalists recognised the role the third sector can play in introducing more diverse and representative stories to the agenda than would likely otherwise be the case.
- Case studies were highly valued by journalists and third sector professionals as a key means to illustrate the significance of poverty news themes in ordinary people's lives and to make news stories more meaningful and relevant for audiences. However, journalists and third sector professionals were also aware that the benefits of participating in case studies were not always clear for the individuals involved.
- Journalists highly valued third sector cooperation in facilitating access to case study participants. However, tensions were also reported in this working relationship, focused mainly on time and resource pressures faced by both professional groups and duty of care/ethical reporting responsibilities towards potential participants.
- The success of journalist–third sector relationships varied with levels of expertise, experience and mutual understanding of professional pressures and priorities. However, there is a unique opportunity in Wales to develop a better, mutually beneficial understanding of the priorities and challenges underpinning one another's work.

Conclusions

There is an encouraging story to tell about news media narratives on poverty in Wales. Our content analysis study demonstrated that, generally, reporting was fair and balanced and seems to reflect the importance attributed by our interviewed journalists to avoiding stigmatising representations of poverty. Ethical considerations in reporting poverty and the potential vulnerability of those experiencing it were foregrounded in many journalists' reflections and they were interested in finding ways to improve the fairness, representativeness and meaningfulness of their reporting. Journalists defined their professional values very much in opposition to the kind of sensationalising coverage and gratuitous scapegoating that we might see elsewhere in the UK news media. The content research has also highlighted how routine pressures and increasingly limited newsroom resources may lead to a gap between reporting ideals and practices on poverty, however. Journalists highlighted how drawing sufficient attention in news to recognise the continuing importance of an ongoing issue like poverty is not easy. Moreover, directly accessing people's stories on the ground and unpacking the complex social implications of official statistics, trends or policy changes are a challenge for journalists without specialist briefs or local connections.

During our monitoring, the Tata Steel crisis and other large businesses running into financial difficulties were prominent stories, and the main issues associated with poverty were unemployment and job insecurity. In some of these reports, informative and in-depth analyses examined why these events had happened, often pointing to structural factors leading to economic vulnerability and uncertainty. Responsibility for poverty was largely, albeit implicitly, attached to government and business, with the Welsh Government, in particular, looked to for a response.

Some reporting featured the consequences for workers and others experiencing poverty, especially in deindustrialised areas. Ordinary citizens were frequently used as sources. However, it was the politicians who were most likely to be heard in the coverage of poverty. Moreover, the gendered nature of journalists' sources was striking, with more than twice as many sources identified as male than female. This may have been, in part, a function of gendered workforces in the industries beset by crisis, but it nonetheless highlights a significant limitation in the diversity of voices and range of poverty experiences highlighted in the news. In the majority of coverage featuring poverty, it was evident that the dynamic of ordinary people's experiences was often lost.

In reporting thematically focused on macroeconomic and political issues, what stories *mean* in people's lives is usually left unexplored. Seldom, in coverage about unemployment, austerity and cuts to social resources, or about major political decisions or campaigns, did narratives unfold that meaningfully connect the political and economic forces at play to how they could impact livelihoods, everyday individual or family experiences, or communities. In the reporting of the EU referendum captured in our sample, for example, leaving or voting to leave the EU was positioned as a more likely cause of poverty than remaining. However, it is notable that this aspect of the coverage did not emerge until well into the referendum campaign, and that usually, such evaluations were introduced by politicians' campaign messages, rather than in-depth journalistic investigation of the potential impacts in people's lives.

Routinely embedded in news driven by politics or business news, there is a risk that poverty may appear as a habitual feature or social condition of Wales's contemporary (or historic) circumstances, rather than be subjected to critical journalistic scrutiny or account. The contextualising factors for poverty are complex. Seemingly dry or specialist policy detail, such as on housing or other social policy, play a role alongside structural forces whose relevance may be difficult to explain and to capture as news. Making such factors relevant and meaningful to audiences requires specialist knowledge, as well as resource intensive storytelling techniques, such as case studies. Conversely, where reports do focus powerfully on everyday lived experiences of poverty, their resonance may not necessarily connect with the complex conditioning or 'framing' features that would explaining causes, consequences or responsibility for poverty in Wales.

The news journalists we interviewed generally recognised that the third sector can play an important role in this space. Indeed, the third sector already plays a role in connecting journalists in Wales with ordinary people's experiences on the ground, extends the range of possibilities for news stories on poverty and introduces journalists to more diverse and representative examples than they would regularly be able to access. However, there remain considerable challenges in how best to productively facilitate this role in practice, and maintain critical professional distance in journalist–third sector media communications relationships. Our research suggests experiences of such relationships vary greatly in levels of expertise, experience and understanding of professional pressures and priorities. The prevailing view amongst those we interviewed from the third sector is that the mainstream news remains of central importance in producing ideas about poverty and conditioning public attitudes towards the people they support. However, their capacity to react and respond to journalists' requests to assist in poverty stories is often restricted by resource, time and expertise limitations.

Indeed, especially for grass-roots service providers, this kind of work may not necessarily be aligned with the core priorities of their organisations and may be considered a costly diversion. Yet, all of our third sector interviewees clearly remained concerned about how the broader public discourse on poverty affected public attitudes, and its tangible impacts upon the climate in which they work. It is also the case that larger and more advocacy-oriented organisations already successfully partner with smaller front-line charities and groups on projects involving media communications.

There is a strong rationale for greater cooperation between third sector organisations working towards shared objectives in media communications. Discussions of our preliminary research findings amongst third sector and news media professionals at our events in April 2017 and November 2018 highlighted the value placed by journalists and the third sector on poverty in a news narrative that is as representative, fair and meaningful as it can be. There is already a co-dependence between third sector communications and news media in reporting poverty. The proximate and relatively 'small' worlds of each sector in Wales also provide a unique opportunity to develop a better, mutually beneficial understanding of the priorities and challenges underpinning one another's work. As such, I recommend our findings in the hope they will be useful to both sectors, encouraging critical reflection, strategic cooperation and a network of understanding about reporting poverty for a more representative, fair and meaningful narrative on poverty in Wales.

Appendices

Appendix A: Keywords in English and in Welsh

English keywords: poverty or economic! or financial or impoverish! or hardship or pinch or privation or penniless or destitut! or 'low income' or 'economic! exclu!' or 'social! exclu! or socially excluded' or margin! or underprivilege! or disadvantage or inequality or poor or 'hard up' or 'depriv!' or penniless or 'global poverty' or rich! or wealth! or privilege! or unemploy! or jobless! or redundan! or jobseeker or homeless! or neets or wage! or 'in work' or austerity or allowance! or 'employment support' or benefit! or 'pension credit!' or pension! or 'bedroom tax' or 'food bank!' or 'job centre' or 'work and pensions' or 'living allowance' or 'income support' or 'universal credit' or 'tax credit' or 'bedroom tax' or 'soup kitchen!' or 'food bank!' or 'azure card!' or charit! or bankrup! or insolven! or debt or indebt! or 'payday loan' or homeless! or 'poor housing' or 'on the streets' or 'living rough' or 'single parent' or 'lone parent' or childcare or fuel or starv! or thrift! or frugal! or 'mak! ends meet' or suffer! or 'personal independence payment!' or 'PIP'

    Welsh keywords: tlodi; economaidd; yn economaidd; ariannol; llymhau; tlodion; dirywiad; caledi; gwasgu; amddifadrwydd; dim; amddifad; amddifedi; incwm isel; gwaharddiad; economaidd; gwaharddiad cymdeithasol; ffiniol; cyrion; difreinticdig; anfantais; anfanteision; anghydraddoldeb; tlawd; amddifad; diffyg; tlodi rhyngwladol; cyfoethog; cyfoeth; ariannog; cefnog; tangyflogaeth; di-waith; digyflog; heb waith; cyflog; cyflogau; cyflogedig; 'mewn gwaith'; llymder; cynildeb; lwfans; lwfansau; lwfansiau; 'cymorth cyflogaeth'; budd; buddion; 'budd pensiwn'; 'buddion pensiwn'; pensiwn; pensiynau; pensiynwr; pensiynwyr; 'treth llofft'; 'banc bwyd'; 'banciau bwyd'; 'canolfan byd gwaith'; 'canolfannau byd gwaith'; 'gwaith a phensiynau'; 'lwfans byw'; 'cymorth incwm'; 'credyd cyffredinol'; 'credyd treth'; 'treth llofft'; 'cegin gawl'; 'ceginau cawl'; 'banc bwyd'; 'banciau bwyd'; 'cardyn azure'; 'cardiau azure'; elusen; elusennau; elusengar; hael; methdalu; methdalwyr; methdaliad; dyledus; 'mewn dyled'; dyled; dyledion; dyledus; dyledusrwydd; 'benthyciad diwrnod cyflog'; 'benthyciadau diwrnod cyflog'; digartref; 'cartrefi gwael'; 'ar y strydoedd'; 'byw ar y stryd'; 'rhiant unigol'; 'rhieni unigol'; 'gofal plant'; tanwydd; newynu; newynog; llwgu; newyn; cynildeb; cynnil; diwastraff; 'dau ben llinyn ynghyd'; dioddef; dioddefaint; dioddefus

Appendix B: Background on content analysis titles and programmes

Newspapers

	Ownership	Readership	Location
Western Mail	Trinity Mirror	19,910 (2015)	Cardiff
Daily Post	Trinity Mirror	25,426 (2015)	Llandudno
Golwg	Welsh Government/ Welsh Book Council		Llanbedr Pont Steffan
Golwg 360	Welsh Government/ Welsh Book Council		Llanbedr Pont Steffan
Carmarthen Journal	Trinity Mirror	12,400 (2014)	Carmarthen
South Wales Argus	Newsquest	13,000	Newport

Television programmes

	Produced by	Time	Hours
Wales Today	BBC Wales	6:30–7:00	20
Newyddion 9	BBC Wales	9:00–9:30	20
Wales Tonight	ITV Wales	6:00–6:30	20

Radio programmes

	Station	Time	Hours
Post Cyntaf	BBC Radio Cymru	7:05–8:05	40
Good Morning Wales	BBC Radio Wales	6:30–7:30	40

Appendix C: Coding scheme

Poverty coverage in the news media in Wales

Media: **TV** (BBC/ITV/S4C) **Radio** (Post Cyntaf/GMW/BridgeFM/CapitalFM)
Print (WesternMail/NWDailyPost/SWArgus/CarmarthenJournal/Golwg)
Online (Wales Online)

Headline:...

Date: [ ][ ][ ][ ] Coding Period (1, 2, 3, 4, 5, 6, 7, 8)

Poverty issue(s): main theme/other

Main theme

Economy	Politics	Europe	Charity (other)	Sport/recreation
Health	Law/order	Foreign policy/ affairs other	Migration	Local government
Education	Security	International aid	Religion	Other

News hook

UK national government report/policy/politics	Experiences of poverty/ social exclusion/ marginalisation	EU referendum	Strike or union protest
Opinion poll related to poverty/social exclusion/ marginalisation	Charity/third sector activity (reports, events, campaigns etc.)	Law and order	Local authority/ council
WAG report/policy/politics	Business	Benefits fraud	Other ....

Poverty-related issues featured

Unemployment	Pensions	Homelessness	Child poverty	Household bills	Inequality
Under-employment	Social/ welfare funding cuts	Poor housing	Hunger	Cost of childcare	Forced labour/ slavery
Low/inadequate wages	Benefit levels (other)	Rent levels	Food banks	Cost of transport	
Debt	Access to benefits (other)		Health problems	Cost of living (general)	
Access to credit				Rural poverty	
				Poor economy/ infrastructure	
				Poverty and deprivation	Other ....

Groups/individuals affected by poverty issues

Single parent(s)	Youth	People with disability	Community/ general public
Parents/families	Retired/elderly	Refugees	
Worker(s)	Military	Migrant background other	Other ....
Not applicable	Women	Homeless people	Not applicable

Location

Cardiff	'Valleys'	Elsewhere in UK ....
Swansea	Other named city/town/region	UK in general
Port Talbot	Wales in general	International
		Other.....................................

Poverty issues experienced by/affecting specific groups (1,2,3 etc. reflecting groups/individuals affected)

Unemployment	Low/inadequate wages	Accessing benefits and services	Homelessness
Employment insecurity	Debt	Poverty/social exclusion/marginalisation (in general)	Other ....
Underemployment	Pension insecurity	Health (mental/physical)	Not applicable

Framing of poverty (values to be determined through pilot study)

Cause(s) of/ reasons for poverty	Consequences of poverty	Attribution of responsibility for poverty	Responses suggested to poverty
Structural (general/other)	Low household incomes/tight budgets	National government policy (present)	National government intervention

Globalisation	Communities suffer	National government policy (past)	WAG intervention
China/India	Children/families suffer	EU policy	Local government intervention
Business practices/ actions of corporations	Health problems	WAG policy	Private org/ business intervention
Wales economy/ deindustrialisation	Educational problems	Local government policy	EU remain vote
Fuel/energy costs	Social exclusion (low attainment other; exclusion from opportunities generally)	Individuals affected	EU leave vote
Transportation problems	Social/economic inequality	Private interests/ business	Political campaign
Voting to leave EU/Brexit	Voting to leave EU	Protest	
Voting to remain in EU/EU membership		Voting to remain in EU	Raise benefit levels
Individual (general/other)			Cut benefit levels
Substance dependence			Raise minimum/ living wage
Worklessness			Charitable project(s)
			Charitable donations
Funding cuts/ austerity			Union action
			Individual action
			Charitable contribution
			Law and order
			Art and culture
Other	Other	Other	Other ....
Not applicable	Not applicable	Not applicable	Not applicable

Sources (male/female/not stated)

Political: UK national	Religious figure/ organisation	Education	Ordinary citizen/ resident affected by poverty/social exclusion/ marginalisation	Ordinary citizen/ resident (other)
Political: Welsh Assembly	Opinion poll	Health	Youth	Unidentified source
Political: Local government	Report	Law and order	Elderly	Unknown source
Political: international	Academic		Single Parent	
Third sector/ charity/NGO	Media		Parent (other)	
Political parties	Business		Homeless	
	Union		Person with migrant background	
			Worker	
			Farmer	Other ....
			Other Unidentified	Not applicable/ none

Appendix D: Brief project outline/consent form for journalists

Exploring the Narrative on Poverty

News Media Narratives and News-Making Practices in Wales

The research will explore current news media coverage of poverty in Wales, including how news stories about poverty are put together, how journalists experience reporting poverty, and the kinds of stories that are newsworthy and why.

The project will also investigate the communications work of NGOs in Wales and their relationships with the news media in the coverage of poverty issues.

We would like to interview journalists and editors to understand the opportunities, constraints and pressures encountered by journalists in the reporting of poverty related issues, either in ordinary daily reporting and/or more considered or feature coverage on poverty. More specifically, this will include asking questions exploring:

- Everyday newsroom routines and experiences of reporting poverty related issues
- Current expectations or understandings about the stories that are likely to be newsworthy about poverty and poverty related issues in Wales
- How institutional roles, responsibilities and ethical considerations in journalism may influence the coverage output on poverty
- The role journalism plays in shaping ideas about poverty in Wales
- The figures or organisations understood to be ideal/valuable sources or perspectives in reporting poverty issues and why
- Potential sources that journalists find difficult to access.
- Relationships between journalists working in Wales and the third sector
- Resources that would be considered useful in terms of story leads/material/background or contextualising information.

The research data gathered from the interviews will be used to inform a report to be published (anticipated timescale for draft publication – Winter 2016) and subsequent academic publications. The report will present an analysis of the interview data, alongside a content study of news coverage of poverty in Wales in both the English and Welsh language news media.

The interviews will be conducted in accordance with the research ethics guidelines of Cardiff University School of Journalism, Media and Cultural Studies (JOMEC), and subject to the approval of the JOMEC Research Ethics Committee. Interviews will be audio recorded and transcribed for analysis and the data stored securely in Cardiff University for 5 years.

All interview responses will be anonymised (unless a preference otherwise is expressed) in the write up of research findings. A consent form will be provided for participants to sign in advance of the interview to signal their consent.

Exploring the Narrative on Poverty in Wales

Interview Consent Form

This consent form relates to a Cardiff University School of Journalism project lead by Dr Kerry Moore, which aims to identify, explore and understand recent and continuing news media narratives and journalistic practices on and surrounding poverty in Wales.

By signing this consent form I agree to the following:

- I have read the project information sheet and understand that I will be asked a series of questions about my professional role and experiences of reporting/editing/producing news about issues surrounding poverty.

- I understand that participation in this study is entirely voluntary and that I can withdraw at any time without giving a reason.
- I understand that I am free to ask any questions at any time.
- I understand that the information I provide will be shared with the research team and may be used in subsequent publications.
- I give my permission for this information to be used (tick one of the following):
  ☐ **Anonymised** (N.B. it is possible that my comments may be identifiable to others even when my name is not used – e.g., due to familiarity with my work or professional role and/or the relatively small pool of potential participants involved in the research and limited geographical area from which they are drawn)
  ☐ **Named** (the information I provide will be identifiable to me)
  ☐ **Named, but with specific sections anonymised** (N.B. I will have the opportunity to review the interview transcript and decide, in conversation with the researcher, which sections should be anonymised and how anonymity is to be enacted)
- I understand that the information provided by me will be held securely at Cardiff University, and, in accordance with the Data Protection Act, will be retained for a period of at least 5 years.
- I, _____ consent to participate in the study conducted by _____ for the School of Journalism, Media & Cultural Studies, Cardiff University.

Signed (researcher):
Signed (Participant):
Date:

Appendix E: Brief project outline/consent form for third sector professionals

Exploring the Narrative on Poverty

Poverty, NGOs and the News Media in Wales

Project Information Sheet
The research will investigate current news media coverage of poverty in Wales, including how news stories about poverty are put together, how journalists experience reporting poverty, and the kinds of stories that are newsworthy and why.

Part of this work involves exploring the communications work of NGOs in Wales, and their relationships with the news media in the coverage of poverty issues. We therefore want to interview NGO Communications Officers and other Third Sector professionals in Wales to explore the opportunities, constraints and pressures faced in their communications practices, and will specifically involve an examination of:

- How Communications Officers and Third Sector professionals seeking to represent the voices of those they support, work.
- How institutional roles, responsibilities and other pressures may influence their practice
- Understandings of the role journalism plays in shaping ideas about poverty in Wales
- The existing relationships people have with the news media in Wales
- Understandings of news values and how journalists construct reports on poverty
- Perceptions of the current news narrative on poverty in recent years
- How, if at all, people have sought to influence that narrative and with what degree of success
- Beliefs about newsworthy stories that are not being told
- Whether there are potential (re)sources for news that reporters do not currently access

The research data gathered from the interviews will be used to inform a report to be published (anticipated timescale for publication – November 2016) and subsequent academic publications. The report will present an analysis of the interview data, alongside an analysis of data from interviews with journalists and editors working in Wales, and data from a content study of news coverage of poverty in Wales in both the English and Welsh language news media.

The interviews will be conducted in accordance with the research ethics guidelines of Cardiff University School of Journalism, Media and Cultural Studies (JOMEC), and subject to the approval of the JOMEC Research Ethics Committee. Interviews will be audio recorded and transcribed for analysis and the data stored securely in Cardiff University for 5 years.

All interview responses will be anonymised (unless a preference otherwise is expressed) in the write up of research findings. A consent form will be provided for participants to sign in advance of the interview to signal their consent.

Exploring the Narrative on Poverty in Wales

Interview Consent Form

This consent form relates to a Cardiff University School of Journalism project lead by Dr Kerry Moore and Dr Sian Powell which aims to identify, explore and understand recent and continuing news media narratives and journalistic practices on and surrounding poverty in Wales.

By signing this consent form I agree to the following:

- I have read the project information sheet and understand that I will be asked a series of questions about my professional role and experiences of engaging with news media in Wales regarding issues surrounding poverty in Wales.
- I understand that participation in this study is entirely voluntary and that I can withdraw at any time without giving a reason.
- I understand that I am free to ask any questions at any time.
- I understand that the information I provide will be shared with the research team and may be used in subsequent publications.
- I give my permission for this information to be used (tick one of the following):
  - ☐ **Anonymised** (N.B. it is possible that my comments may be identifiable to others even when my name is not used – e.g., due to familiarity with my work or professional role and/or the relatively small pool of potential participants involved in the research and limited geographical area from which they are drawn)
  - ☐ **Named** (the information I provide will be identifiable to me)
  - ☐ **Named, but with specific sections anonymised** (N.B. I will have the opportunity to review the interview transcript and decide, in conversation with the researcher, which sections should be anonymised and how anonymity is to be enacted)
- I understand that the information provided by me will be held securely at Cardiff University, and, in accordance with the Data Protection Act, will be retained for a period of at least 5 years.
- I, _____ consent to participate in the study conducted by for the School of Journalism, Media & Cultural Studies, Cardiff University.

Signed (researcher):
Signed (Participant):
Date:

Appendix F: Interview schedules

Exploring the Narrative on Poverty in Wales

Interview Questions for News Media Professionals

Putting stories together
We'd like to start by asking you about how stories on poverty or poverty related issues would normally be put together and your role in that…

- What would normally be your role when there is a story on poverty related issues? Can you walk us through the process and your role in it? (…perhaps starting from how it would usually be assigned?)

- Will there be specific reporters responsible for covering poverty issues – Do you have reporters who are specialists for these issues? Would any journalist who identifies a 'good story' then cover the issue?
- How much time do you usually have to produce a piece?
- How many people would be involved in producing it? What roles do they play?
- How is the story integrated into the news programme/newspaper? (e.g. positioning, editorial intervention during the production process)

Sourcing Stories
We're interested in who has a voice in poverty coverage (which individuals or organisations are used by journalists as sources) and how these voices are accessed…

- Where do you get your stories about poverty or economic inequality from? (e.g., Other media? Press releases? Sources?)
- Do you engage with social media to find organisations, contacts or stories?
- Do you make contact with 3ʳᵈ sector organisations and charities? For what kinds of stories would you look to contact them? How do you tend to do this?
- Which organisations do you tend to think of when putting together a story about poverty? **Are some groups/organisations more difficult to access than others? If so (how) do you try to resolve these kinds of difficulties?**
- How do you choose your sources for stories about poverty issues?
- Do you have regular contacts? What is likely to influence whether you maintain a relationship with them?
- What makes an ideal or valuable source for you in reporting poverty issues and why?
- Who do you think has the expertise/profile to speak on these issues? Who would you call for an opinion/statement?
- Are there any potential sources (people who you would like to use) who you haven't accessed for your stories? Why? What are the impediments?
- If you were trying to ensure a breadth or balance of opinion in reporting poverty related stories, which figures or organisations would you try to include in order to represent different sides of the story? What do you think of as being 'different sides' of the story when it comes to poverty issues in Wales?
- What kinds of information do charities/third sector organisations tend to offer when you contact them about a story? Is this useful? Does it tend to match up with the kinds of material you hoped for?
- Does the quality of information tend to be of a level that is useful? What are the most useful kinds of information? Can you describe an example of when you received very useful information, or when contact with a charity/third sector organisation led to a story that in your view was very strong?

- How about an experience of contacting or interacting with a third sector organisation that was less successful? Can you describe and example or generally reflect upon when and why things haven't worked well?
- How do you think relationships between 3rd sector organisations and journalists/the news media could be improved?

Newsworthiness of poverty/poverty related issues

We'd like to ask you now about the stories to be told about poverty and poverty related issues in Wales and when they make the news...

- What do you consider to be currently the big stories relating to poverty or economic inequality in Wales? (that affect Wales or people in Wales)
- In your view, are these the types of stories that are most frequently reported about poverty, economic inequality and economically disadvantaged/marginalised people in Wales? If not, what stories are?
- What do you think are the main issues associated in those stories with poverty?
- How would you define 'poverty'?
- Which individuals/groups do you think are mostly identified as experiencing poverty/social marginalisation/exclusion?
- How, if at all, do you think these things have changed in recent months and years? In your experience as a (reporter/editor/producer) do you believe poverty to be more or less newsworthy now?
- How well do you think the news media (generally in Wales) contextualise poverty and poverty related issues (e.g., in terms of the reasons outlined for poverty, the attribution of responsibility for it, the kinds of solutions suggested or consequences of poverty that are explained)
- When do you/your organisation cover poverty issues? What makes them newsworthy for you? (i.e., how and why does an ongoing issue such as poverty become news)
- What status do these stories tend have in the overall newsroom agenda?

Public Audience Opinion

- Where do you think public opinion is on poverty and/or economic inequality? What do you imagine people are thinking about it in Wales (e.g., in terms of what it is/what it looks like, its causes, consequences)?
- Does this differ from your particular audience's opinion?

Depicting Poverty

I'd like to ask you something about how you go about depicting poverty and poverty related issues now...

- In terms of visual representations... Are there any particular difficulties you might face in illustrating poverty stories (e.g., in selecting images to illustrate poverty, or in producing relevant footage)?

- We've noticed that often graphics are used... what leads to or informs a decision to use graphics and how are these images selected?
- Can you tell us about the kind of message you are trying to convey when using these types of images?
- What are your considerations when featuring people who are experiencing poverty or issues relating to economic inequality in your reports? Are there specific newsroom guidelines you follow?
- Are there stories that you feel you have to cover, even if you'd rather not? (E.g. new government policy).
- How much pressure (if any) do you feel (or do you think news organisations in general might feel) to cover the agenda of particular departments, parties, politicians or organisations? Are there any examples you could tell us about?
- Are there issues about poverty or economic inequality that you consider 'the great untold story'? Why do you think no one is telling it?
- Do you think there is (or has ever) been an avoidance of talking about poverty in the news in Wales? Why might this be/have been the case?
- Is there any difficulty in terms of terminology? Are there terms labelling poverty or people experiencing it that you would like to use but cannot or don't feel you can for any reason? Are there any preferred terms?
- Are there any social groups and/or areas of the country that you associate most with stories about poverty at the moment? Do you think there are any groups/places that receive more or less attention than they should?
- Can you tell us about a poverty story in Wales that you have covered recently that you think was particularly important? (...why did you cover it in this way? What did you learn from it? Is there anything you would have liked to do differently?)
- Have you covered any stories related to these issues with a focus beyond Wales/an international focus?
- What do you think is the role or responsibility (perhaps) of the news media is in Wales in covering poverty or economic inequality? What role do you think journalism plays in shaping ideas about poverty in Wales?
- Have you ever been or felt challenged on how you have represented poverty, or how you have featured an organisation and its views on the issue? If so, can you tell us about it?

Three of the big stories that have happened during our project are...
Story: 1) Steel, 2) Assembly Election, or 3) EU Referendum/Brexit

  o Did you report on any of these stories? Can you tell us about how you reported the story? Was poverty/income inequality a particular focus or concern for your piece? Why/why not?
  o (N.B. If not asked earlier...) Can you tell us about the most memorable story about poverty you have covered?

○ If any other questions come up as our research progresses that we haven't asked today but which seem to us to be very important, would you be happy for us to contact you, perhaps by email, to follow up?

Wrapping up...

○ Finally, we'd like to ask you about any measures (or resources perhaps) that you think might help you in reporting the important stories related to poverty in Wales...
○ What would be useful or valuable to you – for example, in looking for story leads, in strengthening or improve your network of sources, in accessing background or contextualising information or other important material? (...suggest we might follow up on that question in correspondence perhaps?)
○ Is there anything else you would like to talk about that we haven't covered?

Later/follow up:
Our plan: networking events

1) Closed event for third sector workers and journalists and editors
2) Public event
   ○ What kind of discussions or topics would be useful to you?
   ○ Is there any particular information (or training?) that you think would be useful?
   ○ Do you have suggestions for people you would like to see invited? (Follow up)
   ○ We'll be devising the format of these events over the next few months. Any input from you would be great – please be in touch. We will also keep you updated of our findings.

Exploring the Narrative on Poverty in Wales

Interview Questions with Third Sector Organisations

Tell me about the organisation and your role here

○ Are you the person who always communicates with the media?
○ How many people are involved in external communications within your organisation?
○ Has there been any training or support in your organisation around communications?

Tell us about your practices and organisational structure around communications

○ Walk me through the process for a story from your organisation to the media. Who makes decisions around stories? (Final approval, editorial process?)

o What do you already do?

o How do you use press releases, newsletters, blogs, social media?

o What kinds of relationships do you have with journalists and media organisations? Is so, how do these develop?

o How do you think your communications are working? Is it working well? Is there anything that isn't working so well?

o Could you give me some examples of recent stories or how you have tried to communicate your work?

Your news values (when, why is something a story?)

o How do you decide that you have a story that you want to share? Why?

o How do you decide when to bring a story to the media? For example, with your projects, do you tend to have a communications plan? Do you ever respond to stories in the news?

o Are there specific times of the year when you have stories that you want to get out there?

o What do you think makes something a good story?

o How do you get your information for these stories?

o What do you see as the most important story that you have shared successfully?

o Is there an example of an important story that was not successful?

o What do you think journalists think makes something a good story?

Goals for media coverage

o What do you hope to achieve through media stories?

o Who do you have in mind as your audience? Is that always clear? Does anything change in your approach when your audience is different (i.e. policy makers, public?)

o How do you hope media coverage will support your work?

o What would be the perfect scenario for you in terms of media relationships or coverage?

o Can you tell us about the most memorable story about poverty you have shared?

Role as mediator, representation (between service users and media/ public)

o How do you bring the voices and experiences of your services users to the media?

o Do you encounter any challenges or difficulties around this? (e.g., How do you handle issues of confidentiality, voices heard directly, etc.?)

o Are there any issues or groups you work with whose stories are difficult to tell for some reason?

○ Are there typical stories about your service users that you see often? Examples (…)?

Views and beliefs around poverty

○ How do you define poverty?
○ When you think of poverty in Wales, what comes to mind?
○ Which individuals/groups do you think are mostly identified as experiencing poverty/social marginalisation/exclusion?
○ What do you think are the causes of poverty in Wales? Why is poverty an issue here?
○ What do you think your organisation's role is in addressing poverty in Wales?
○ How does the role of your organisation link with those of other agencies – i.e., do aim to work in conjunction with other third sector organisations, with government, with the media perhaps … to achieve your goals?

Portrayal of poverty in the media

○ What role do you think the media have in shaping narratives of poverty in Wales?
○ How do you feel that poverty is currently being depicted in the Welsh media? (e.g. is accuracy an issue? Breadth? Detail? Attention? Distribution of media coverage across Wales? Any other issues?)
○ Is this different in Wales compared to the rest of the UK media?

We'd like to turn now to ask you your opinion about the stories to be told about poverty and poverty related issues in Wales and when they make the news…

• What do you consider to be currently the big stories relating to poverty or economic inequality in Wales? (that affect Wales or people in Wales)
• In your view, are these the types of stories that are most frequently reported about poverty, economic inequality and economically disadvantaged/ marginalised people in Wales? If not, what stories are?
• What do you think are the main issues associated in those stories with poverty?
• How, if at all, do you think these things have changed in recent months and years? In your experience as a professional working in the third sector, do you believe poverty to be more or less newsworthy now?
• How well do you think the news media (generally in Wales) contextualise poverty and poverty related issues (e.g., in terms of the reasons outlined for poverty, the attribution of responsibility for it, the kinds of solutions suggested or consequences of poverty that are explained?)

- When do you/your organisation try to gain coverage for poverty issues? What makes them newsworthy for you? (i.e., how and why does an ongoing issue such as poverty become an important story for publication/news)

Public perceptions of poverty

- What do you think the public perception of poverty and/or income inequality is in Wales? What do you imagine people are thinking about it in Wales (e.g., in terms of what it is/what it looks like, its causes, consequences)?
  o Is this in line with news media representations? Do you see any other influences?
  o Does this differ from how the people you represent/your client base/ service users see poverty do you think?
  o Do you think *this* is different in Wales compared to the rest of the UK? What's your feeling?

Turning back to your organisation now...
Portrayal of your organisation in the media

  o How do you think the media view your organisation? Do you think they understand your aims?
  o Have you ever felt like your projects or the issues you have tried to raise have been misrepresented in the past? Could you tell us about an example?
  o Is there anything we are missing that is a serious impediment for you to getting these stories out there?

Story: 1) Steel, 2) Assembly Election, or 3) EU Referendum/Brexit

  o Did you try to get any related stories out around this news story? Why or why not? How did it go?
  o If you did try to put the story out there, do you mind me asking where you tried to put it?
  o (N.B. If not asked earlier...) Can you tell us about the most memorable story about poverty you have shared?
  o Is there anything else you would like to talk about?
  o If any other questions come up as our research progresses that we haven't asked today but which seem to us to be very important, would you be happy for us to contact you, perhaps by email, to follow up?

Later/follow up:
Our plan: networking events

  1) Closed event for third sector workers and journalists and editors
  2) Public event
     o What kind of discussions or topics would be useful to you?

- ○ Is there any particular information or training that you think would be useful?
- ○ Do you have suggestions for people you would like to see invited? (Follow up)
- ○ We'll be devising the format of these events over the next few months. Any input from you would be great – please be in touch. We will also keep you updated of our findings.

Reference List

Armstrong, S. (2017). *The new poverty*. London, New York: Verso.

Barnard, H. (2018). *Poverty in Wales*. Retrieved from https://www.jrf.org.uk/report/poverty-wales-2018

Barton, C., & Hough, D. (2016). *Fuel poverty*. Retrieved from House of Commons Library: http://researchbriefings.parliament.uk/ResearchBriefing/Summary/SN05115#fullreport

Bauman, Z. (2004). *Wasted lives: Modernity and its outcasts*. Cambridge: Polity Press.

Baumberg, B., Bell, K., Gaffney, D., Deacon, R., Hood, C., & Sage, D. (2013). *Benefits stigma in Britain*. Retrieved from https://wwwturn2us-2938.cdn.hybridcloudspan.com/T2UWebsite/media/Documents/Benefits-Stigma-in-Britain.pdf

BBC News. (2016, 13 December). No end to child poverty by 2020, Welsh Government says. *BBC News Online*. Retrieved from http://www.bbc.co.uk/news/uk-wales-politics-38308763

Bevan Foundation. (2010). *Poverty and social exclusion in Wales*. Ebbw Vale, Wales: Bevan Foundation. Retrieved from https://www.bevanfoundation.org/publications/poverty-and-social-exclusion-in-wales-2/

Bevan Foundation. (2016). *Prosperity without poverty: A framework for action in Wales*. Retrieved from https://www.bevanfoundation.org//wp-content/uploads/2016/11/Prosperity-without-poverty.pdf

Bevan Foundation. (2018). *Tough times ahead? What 2018 might hold for Wales*. Retrieved from Merthyr Tydfil, UK: https://www.bevanfoundation.org/publications/tough-times-ahead/

Blom, J. N., & Hansen, K. R. (2015). Click bait: Forward-reference as lure in online news headlines. *Journal of Pragmatics, 76*, 87–100. doi: https://doi.org/10.1016/j.pragma.2014.11.010

Bloodworth, J. (2016). *The myth of meritocracy: Why working-class kids still get working-class jobs*. London: Biteback Publishing.

Bourdieu, P. (1996). *On television*. New York: The New York Press.

Bourdieu, P. (2012 (1984)). *Distinction*. London, New York: Routledge.

Chouliaraki, L. (2006). *The spectatorship of suffering*. London, Thousand Oaks, CA, New Delhi: Sage.

Chouliaraki, L. (2013). *The ironic spectator: Solidarity in the age of post-human-itarianism*. Cambridge: Polity.

Church Action on Poverty & National Union of Journalists. (2016). NUJ guide to reporting poverty. Retrieved from https://www.nuj.org.uk/documents/nuj -guide-to-reporting-poverty

Clery, A. (2013). *Public attitudes to poverty and welfare 1983–2011*. Retrieved from http://natcen.ac.uk/our-research/research/public-attitudes-to-poverty -and-welfare-1983-2011

Crossley, S. (2017). *In their place: The imagined geographies of poverty*. London: Pluto Press.

Cushion, S., Kilby, A., Thomas, R., Morani, M., & Sambrook, R. (2018). News-papers, impartiality and television news. *Journalism Studies, 19*(2), 162–181. doi: https://doi.org/10.1080/1461670X.2016.1171163

Davies, N. (2011). *Flat earth news: An award-winning reporter exposes false-hood, distortion and propaganda in the global media*. London: Vintage.

Department for Business Energy and Industrial Strategy. (2017). *Annual fuel poverty statistics report, 2017 (2015 Data)*. Retrieved from https://www.gov .uk/government/uploads/system/uploads/attachment_data/file/639118 /Fuel_Poverty_Statistics_Report_2017_revised_August.pdf

Department for Work and Pensions. (2016). Guidance: How low income is measured in households below average income. Retrieved from https:// www.gov.uk/government/publications/how-low-income-is-measured /text-only-how-low-income-is-measured

Eurobarometer. (2010). *Poverty and social exclusion report*. Retrieved from http://ec.europa.eu/commfrontoffice/publicopinion/archives/ebs/ebs _355_en.pdf

Fitzpatrick, S., Pawson, H., Bramley, G., Wilcox, S., Watts, B., & Wood, J. (2017). *The homelessness monitor: Wales 2017*. Retrieved from https://www.crisis .org.uk/media/237651/the_homelessness_monitor_wales_2017_es.pdf

Franklin, B., & Murphy, D. (1991). *What news?: The market, politics and the local press*. London: Routledge.

Franklin, B., & Richardson, J. (2002). A journalist's duty? Continuity and change in local newspaper reporting of recent UK general elections. *Journalism Studies, 3*(1), 35–52. doi: https://doi.org/10.1080/14616700120107329

Golding, P., & Middleton, S. (1982). *Images of Welfare: Press and Public Attitudes to Poverty*. Oxford, UK: Robertson & Company.

Goodwin, M., & Heath, O. (2016). *Brexit vote explained: Poverty, low skills and lack of opportunities*. Retrieved from https://www.jrf.org.uk/report/brexit -vote-explained-poverty-low-skills-and-lack-opportunities

Goodwin, S. (2018). Food poverty: What we don't know. Retrieved from http:// endhungeruk.org/food-poverty-dont-know

Gordon, A., Mack, J., Lansley, S., Main, G., Nandy, S., Patsios, D., & Pomati, M. (2013). *The impoverishment of the UK PSE UK first results: Living standards*. Retrieved from http://www.poverty.ac.uk/sites/default/files/attachments

/The_Impoverishment_of_the_UK_PSE_UK_first_results_summary_report_March_28.pdf

Hanitzsch, T., & Vos, T. P. (2018). Journalism beyond democracy: A new look into journalistic roles in political and everyday life. *Journalism, 19*(2), 146–164. doi: https://doi.org/10.1177/1464884916673386

Harcup, T., & O'Neill, D. (2017). What is news? *Journalism Studies, 18*(12), 1470–1488. doi: https://doi.org/10.1080/1461670X.2016.1150193

Hirsch, D. (2007). *Experiences of poverty and educational disadvantage.* Joseph Rowntree Foundation. Retrieved from https://www.jrf.org.uk/report/experiences-poverty-and-educational-disadvantage?gclid=EAIaIQobChMIw_OqspPm6gIViLbtCh3I-AnZEAAYASAAEgJJX_D_BwE

House of Commons Work and Pensions Select Committee. (2017, 21 February). Universal Credit rollout: Inquiry re-launched.

ITV News. (2018, 19 February). Police investigating death of homeless 19-year-old in Cardiff. *ITV News.* Retrieved from http://www.itv.com/news/wales/2018-02-19/police-investigating-death-of-homeless-19-year-old-in-cardiff

Jenkins, J., & Nielsen, R. K. (2019). Proximity, public service, and popularity: A comparative study of how local journalists view quality news. *Journalism Studies, 21*(2), 236–253. doi: https://doi.org/10.1080/1461670X.2019.1636704

Jones, O. (2011). *Chavs: The demonization of the working class.* London, New York: Verso.

Kuiken, J., Schuth, A., Spitters, M., & Marx, M. (2017). Effective headlines of newspaper articles in a digital environment. *Digital Journalism, 5*(10), 1300–1314. doi: https://doi.org/10.1080/21670811.2017.1279978

Lansley, S., & Mack, J. (2015). *Breadline Britain: The rise of mass poverty.* London: One World.

Lewis, J., & Cushion, S. (2019). Think tanks, television news and impartiality. *Journalism Studies, 20*(4), 480–499. doi: https://doi.org/10.1080/14616 70X.2017.1389295

Lister, R. (2004). *Poverty.* Cambridge and Malden, MA: Polity Press.

Littler, J. (2018). *Against meritocracy: Culture, power and myths of mobility.* London: Routledge.

Macdonald, M. (1998). Personalisation in current affairs journalism. *Javnost - The Public, 5*(3), 109–126. doi: https://doi.org/10.1080/13183222.1998.11008686

Marsh, A., Barker, K., Ayrton, C., Treanor, M., & Haddad, M. (2017). *Poverty: The facts* (6 ed.). London: Child Poverty Action Group.

McCombs, M. (2004). *Setting the agenda: The mass media and public opinion.* Cambridge, Malden, MA: Polity.

McGuinness, F. (2018). *Poverty in the UK: Statistics.* Retrieved from https://commonslibrary.parliament.uk/research-briefings/sn07096/#:~:text=How%20many%20people%20are%20in,level%20to%20the%20year%20before

Meijer, I. C. (2001). The public quality of popular journalism: Developing a normative framework. *Journalism Studies, 2*(2), 189–205. doi: https://doi.org/10.1080/14616700120042079

Ministry of Housing Communities and Local Government. (2018). *Rough sleeping statistics, autumn 2017, England*. Retrieved from https://www.gov .uk/government/uploads/system/uploads/attachment_data/file/676097 /Rough_Sleeping_Autumn_2017_Statistical_Release.pdf

Molyneux, L., & Coddington, M. (2019). Aggregation, clickbait and their effect on perceptions of journalistic credibility and quality. *Journalism Practice*, 1–18. doi: https://doi.org/10.1080/17512786.2019.1628658

Mosalski, R. (2017, 29 November). A 32-year-old woman has been found dead in a Cardiff park. *Wales Online*. Retrieved from https://www.walesonline .co.uk/news/wales-news/32-year-old-woman-been-13968902

Nielsen, R. K. (2015). *Local journalism: The decline of newspapers and the rise of digital media*. London, New York: I. B. Tauris.

ONS.(2017).PersistentpovertyintheUKandEU:2015.Retrievedfromhttps://www .ons.gov.uk/peoplepopulationandcommunity/personalandhouseholdfinances /incomeandwealth/articles/persistentpovertyintheukandeu/2015

Pemberton, S., Fahmy, E., Sutton, E., & Bell, K. (2017). Endless pressure: Life on a low income in austere times. *Social Policy & Administration, 51*(7), 1156–1173. doi: https://doi.org/10.1111/spol.12233

Press Association. (2018, 12 February). DWP spent £100m on disability benefit appeals, figures reveal. *Guardian*. Retrieved from https://www.theguardian .com/politics/2018/feb/12/disability-benefit-appeals-department-for-work -and-pensions-figures

Redden, J. (2011). Poverty in the news: A framing analysis of coverage in Canada and the UK. *Information Communication and Society, 14*(6), 820–849. doi: https://doi.org/10.1080/1369118x.2011.586432

Robert, M., Shildrick, T., & Furlong, A. (2014). In search of 'intergenerational cultures of worklessness': Hunting the Yeti and shooting zombies. *Critical Social Policy, 34*(2), 199–220. doi: https://doi.org/10.1177/0261018313501825

Rowe, D. (2011). Obituary for the newspaper? Tracking the tabloid. *Journalism, 12*(4), 449–466. doi: https://doi.org/10.1177/1464884910388232

Schneider, B. (2013). Reporting homelessness. *Journalism Practice, 7*(1), 47–61. doi: https://doi.org/10.1080/17512786.2012.686783

Seymour, D. (2009). *Reporting poverty in the UK: A practical guide for journalists*. York: Joseph Rowntree Foundation, Society of Editors and The Media Trust.

Statistics for Wales. (2017a). Household below average income by year. Retrieved from https://statswales.gov.wales/Catalogue/Community-Safety -and-Social-Inclusion/Poverty/householdbelowaverageincome-by-year

Statistics for Wales. (2017b). *National Rough Sleeper Count, November 2016 – Experimental Statistics* Retrieved from: https://gov.wales/sites/default /files/statistics-and-research/2019-04/national-rough-sleeper-count -november-2016.pdf

Tenenboim, O., & Cohen, A. A. (2015). What prompts users to click and comment: A longitudinal study of online news. *Journalism, 16*(2), 198–217. doi: https://doi.org/10.1177/1464884913513996

Threadgold, T., Clifford, S., Harb, Z., Jewell, J., Powell, V., & Jiang, X. (2007). *Constructing community in South-East Wales.* Cardiff: Joseph Rowntree Foundation.

Tinson, A., Ayrton, C., Barker, K., Born, T. B., Aldridge, H., & Kenway, P. (2016). *Monitoring poverty and social exclusion.* Retrieved from https://www.jrf.org.uk/report/monitoring-poverty-and-social-exclusion-2016

Townsend, P. (1979). *Poverty in the United Kingdom.* London: Allen Lane and Penguin Books.

Tyler, I. (2013). *Revolting subjects: Social abjection and resistance in neoliberal Britain.* London: Zed Books.

UK Government. (2017). Homelessness Reduction Act. Retrieved from http://www.legislation.gov.uk/ukpga/2017/13/pdfs/ukpga_20170013_en.pdf

Volmert, A., Pineau, M., & Kendall-Taylor, N. (2017). *Talking about poverty: How experts and the public understand UK poverty.* Retrieved from https://www.jrf.org.uk/report/talking-about-poverty-how-experts-and-public-understand-uk-poverty

Wacquant, L. (2008). *Urban outcasts: A comparative sociology of advanced marginality.* Cambridge, Malden, MA: Polity.

Wahl-Jorgensen, K. (2018). *Emotions, media and politics.* Cambridge, Medford, MA: Polity.

www.ingramcontent.com/pod-product-compliance
Lightning Source LLC
Chambersburg PA
CBHW071029280326
41935CB00011B/1505